ORTHO

INDOOR & OUTDOOR LIGHTING SOLUTIONS

Meredith® Books
Des Moines, Iowa

Ortho® Books
An imprint of Meredith® Books

Indoor & Outdoor Lighting Solutions
Editor: Larry Johnston
Writer: Daniel Blitzer
Senior Associate Design Director: Tom Wegner
Assistant Editor: Harijs Priekulis
Copy Chief: Terri Fredrickson
Copy and Production Editor: Victoria Forlini
Editorial Operations Manager: Karen Schirm
Managers, Book Production: Pam Kvitne,
    Marjorie J. Schenkelberg
Contributing Copy Editor: Steve Hallam
Technical Proofreader: Emily Mead
Contributing Proofreaders: Julie Cahalan, Sara Henderson,
    David Krause
Indexer: Barbara L. Klein
Electronic Production Coordinator: Paula Forest
Editorial and Design Assistant: Renee E. McAtee,
    Karen McFadden

**Additional Editorial Contributions from
    Art Rep Services**
Director: Chip Nadeau
Designer: lk Design
Illustrator: Dave Brandon

Meredith® Books
Publisher and Editor in Chief: James D. Blume
Design Director: Matt Strelecki
Managing Editor: Gregory H. Kayko
Executive Editor, Gardening and Home Improvement:
    Benjamin W. Allen
Executive Editor, Home Improvement: Larry Erickson

Director, Operations: George A. Susral
Director, Production: Douglas M. Johnston
Executive Director, Sales: Ken Zagor

Vice President and General Manager: Douglas J. Guendel

Meredith Publishing Group
President, Publishing Group: Stephen M. Lacy
Vice President-Publishing Director: Bob Mate

Meredith Corporation
Chairman and Chief Executive Officer: William T. Kerr

Chairman of the Executive Committee: E.T. Meredith III

Photographers
    (Photographers credited may retain copyright ©
    to the listed photographs.)
L = Left, R = Right, C = Center, B = Bottom, T = Top
King Au/Studio Au: 21, 98
Pamela Barkentin-Blackburn: 44BR
J.L. Curtis: 60 Both
deGennaro Associates: 48, 50, 54
Tim Fields: 7TR
D. Randolph Foulds: 13B
GE Lighting: 23, 30, 32, 34, 35, 39, 46 Both, 56
Susan Gilmore: 5, 43, 66, 70TR
Ed Gohlich: 37
Jay Graham: 14B
Jim Hedrich/Hedrich-Blessing: 4, 64B
Hopkins Assoc.: 41, 45
Roy Inman: 70B
Michael Jensen: 6, 11T, 14CL, 58
Jon Jensen: 11B
Jay Johnson: 28
Larry Johnston: 82, 86BL, 87, 92, 94BL, 103BR
Jenifer Jordan: 10, 12, 44BL
Mark Lohman: 68TL
Andy Lyons: 29, 78, 81
Barbara Elliot Martin: 62
Jon Miller/Hedrich-Blessing: 14CR, 49B, 52, 68TR
Michael McKinley: 74, 84B
Jeff McNamara: 70TL
Lark Smothermon/Woolly Bugger Studios: 84T
William Stites: 13T
Tom McWilliam: 40
Eric Roth: 64TR
Rick Taylor: 8
James Yochum Photography: 42, 64TL
Zane Williams: 7TL, 16, 17, 18, 24, 86, 97

Cover photograph: Michael Jensen

All of us at Ortho® Books are dedicated to providing you
with the information and ideas you need to enhance your
home and garden. We welcome your comments and
suggestions about this book. Write to us at:
    Meredith Corporation
    Ortho Books
    1716 Locust St.
    Des Moines, IA 50309–3023

If you would like to purchase any of our home improvement,
gardening, cooking, crafts, or home decorating and design
books, check wherever quality books are sold. Or visit us at:
meredithbooks.com

If you would like more information on other Ortho
products, call 800-225-2883 or visit us at: www.ortho.com

Note to the Readers: Due to differing conditions, tools,
and individual skills, Meredith Corporation assumes no
responsibility for any damages, injuries suffered, or losses
incurred as a result of following the information published
in this book. Before beginning any project, review the
instructions carefully, and if any doubts or questions remain,
consult local experts or authorities. Because codes and
regulations vary greatly, you always should check with
authorities to ensure that your project complies with all
applicable local codes and regulations. Always read and
observe all of the safety precautions provided by
manufacturers of any tools, equipment, or supplies,
and follow all accepted safety procedures.

Lights in, on, and around this gazebo make it look festive at night. Lights in the risers of the steps leading up to the gazebo accent the steps and make them safer.

Lights along a sidewalk mark the way to the front entryway, which is bright and welcoming. The lights along the path are themselves attractive landscape elements.

LIGHTING IN OUR LIVES

Electric lighting has become so universal and trouble-free in American households that most people now take it for granted. That's why many homeowners don't think about the importance of good lighting to home comfort and decorating.

This chapter tells how proper lighting can bring out colors more accurately and create moods in your rooms. Later chapters explain how to design lighting schemes inside and outside your home and how to install the fixtures and controls that can create just the right lighting.

Comfortable lighting in this sitting room combines with sparkling lights in the tree outside the French doors to make an inviting place for a chat or to sit and read.

FUNCTIONAL AND BEAUTIFUL LIGHTING

Good lighting is functional and beautiful. Functional lighting helps you perform tasks throughout the house, enables you to move around in safety, enhances security, and contributes to your enjoyment of your surroundings.

Beautiful lighting adds sparkle and glow to the home. It reveals the beauty of furnishings and establishes a mood: festive, dramatic, relaxed, or simply comfortable and secure.

Exterior and landscape lighting are also important parts of an overall lighting plan for your home.

A combination of lighting techniques usually gives the best results, as in this kitchen.

LOOK AT LIGHTING

Lighting involves both practical and aesthetic considerations, but it is not technically complex. When you start thinking about the lighting scheme for a new home, a major renovation, or a limited redecorating project, look around at friends' homes or even restaurants and shops. Think about the lighting scenes and situations that you like. Then as you read this book, consider your preferences and goals as you start designing lighting that's ideal for your home.

By illuminating the walls to highlight the hanging hats and the floral arrangement on the console, lighting makes this narrow hall more interesting.

Lighting the wall behind the tree accents the tree and prevents dark shadows in the corner.

TWO LIGHTING CHALLENGES

Lighting design revolves around two basic considerations:

■ How can lighting enhance the beauty, atmosphere, and functionality of my home?

■ How do I achieve the results I want?

This book will help you develop an idea of the lighting effects you want and show you how to select and install the equipment that produces those effects.

A VISUAL VOCABULARY

Lighting affects what you see—and often, what you feel. In these pages you will learn a lighting vocabulary to describe the effects you want. And you can follow a simple step-by-step approach to design the lighting for your home.

Looking through the recommendations for indoor and outdoor lighting, you can choose among various options for specific lighting situations. You will find that designing lighting for your home is easy and fun to do. In many cases, you can quickly and easily install the fixtures and controls needed to accomplish your plan yourself.

A LOOK AT LIGHT

Light lets you see the people, objects, and spaces around you. To see them the way you want to, you must be able to describe lighting effects and equipment. With this lighting vocabulary, you can discuss the lighted environment you want, as well as the light sources, fixtures, and controls that will create those effects.

VISION: LIGHT AND COLOR

Vision begins when light reflects off an object, enters the eye, and stimulates receptors on the retina at the back of the eye. Nerve endings send the retina's signals to the brain, which decodes them. So vision involves the light, the object, the eye, and the brain. Visual perceptions depend on all four elements.

Lighting must show the true colors day and night when color is a key style element.

INTENSITY AND COLOR

Light, a form of energy, can be described by its intensity and color. *Intensity* describes how much light a source emits and how much ultimately reaches an object. The more light that reaches an object, the brighter it will look, compared to what is around it.

LIGHT CONTAINS COLOR: White light combines light of all colors. You see color in objects when they reflect light of that color to your eye. Under white light, an apple looks red because it reflects the red component of white light to your eye. Under blue light, the apple looks black because there is no red component to reflect. This principle becomes important when selecting light sources to flatter people, fabrics, finishes, and furnishings in your home.

REFLECTIVITY

The surfaces of objects reflect different amounts of light in different ways. The amount of light an object reflects is determined by its *reflectivity*, a measure of how much of the light that strikes a surface bounces back. (See the chart, *opposite*.) Light that is not reflected is absorbed. Dark surfaces absorb more light than lighter ones. Since light is a form of energy, absorbed light turns into heat—the reason a black car sitting in the sun feels warmer than a white one.

Textured objects, such as a stone wall or napped fabric, absorb more light than flat, smooth surfaces because the recesses of the textures trap light.

Light reflects off polished or shiny surfaces in one direction and at the same angle as it hits, creating an image of the light source. This is how a mirror works and is called *specular reflection*. Shiny surfaces look very bright when viewed in one direction, but appear dark when viewed from other directions. Matte surfaces reflect light in all directions and look bright from all angles. Understanding this principle helps when considering how to place lighting around objects.

Pure white light contains all the colors of the visible spectrum. You can see a particular color in an object only if the light illuminating the object contains that color.

PERCEPTION AND THE HUMAN EYE

When light strikes the retina in the rear of the eye, it stimulates receptors. Some receptors are sensitive to the high intensity and color seen during the day. Others are more sensitive to low light levels, so they are more important at night. That's why people see differently in daylight than at night. This difference in vision is important when considering how to light exterior pathways and patios.

Your brain measures an object's brightness in relation to its surroundings—its *contrast*—rather than as an absolute level of light. Your brain uses your immediate surroundings as the standard value for making contrast measurements of intensity and color. This lets you see effectively in either bright or dim conditions.

Eyes change as people age. They admit less light and change shape, altering vision. Lighting that young people find generous and comfortable often seems both inadequate and glary to people 50 years old or older.

REFLECTIVITY

	White
90% Ultra reflective reflective white paint	10% Black
80% Ordinary white paint and ceiling tiles, white paper	20% Black
70% Off-white paint and laminates	30% Black
	40% Black
50% Light oak, lighter pastels and bright colors	50% Black
	60% Black
30% Light-colored floors and carpets, wall coverings, darker drapes, most woods	70% Black
	80% Black
10% Dark-colored paint, walnut paneling, dark carpet	90% Black
1% Black paint, ink	Solid Black

LIGHTING EFFECTS

We talk about lighting in terms that describe the character of light and tell how it reveals the people, objects, and spaces it illuminates. Many of the descriptions in this section are subjective—they don't refer to precise, measurable quantities. You'll instinctively understand many terms and descriptions as you read them.

BEAMS AND WASHES

The direction and intensity of light determines how we see the form of an object. A concentrated *beam* of light reveals form and texture, creating defining highlights and shadows. A diffused *wash* of light illuminates evenly to reduce shadows, often making objects look flat. A *floodlight* is a less concentrated beam that covers a larger area and creates softer shadows.

DIRECT OR INDIRECT LIGHT

Direct light illuminates a surface without reflecting off another surface. It brightens that object more than its surroundings. The more concentrated the direct light, the more intense a beam it produces. Direct light can also produce a wash or a flood. Direct lighting is usually overhead (downlighting) or from the side.

Indirect light reflects off the ceiling, wall, or other surface before reaching an object. The reflecting surface, such as the ceiling, is generally brighter than the objects or other surfaces lighted indirectly. Most indirect lighting creates a soft wash.

GLOW

WASH

BEAM

The pendant fixture lights this room directly and indirectly. The translucent shade on the table lamp creates a glow; an opaque shade directs most of the floor lamp's light downward.

CONTRAST AND UNIFORMITY

Highlights made by a beam of light create contrast by illuminating all or part of an object or space, leaving unlit areas relatively dim. The part that light touches stands out; the rest recedes in your perception.

A wash or flood spreads light across a surface evenly so you see it all in a *uniform* light. Lights installed throughout a room create an overall uniform effect. The light does not have to be perfectly equal from all sources to seem even.

SPARKLE AND GLOW

Think of *sparkle* as the intriguing play of light on droplets of water, polished silverware, or faceted crystal. Sparkle suggests festivity and formality. Tiny, flickering points of light themselves become further sources of sparkle.

Glow is the soft spread of light from a luminous object, such as a dimmed lightbulb or a linen lampshade. Light falling on china, fabric, or a painting creates a glowing pool of pleasant brightness.

GLARE

A light source that's too big and too bright creates *glare*. An unshaded light can also cause glare; avoid using a bare light source unless it produces very little light or is dimmed to a low intensity. A translucent glass, plastic, or fabric diffuser softens the light and prevents glare. An opaque shade or housing in front of the source blocks the light and keeps the beam from glaring directly into people's eyes.

Cove lighting above the cabinets, countertop lighting under the cabinets, and ceiling lights combine to minimize shadows and fill this kitchen with uniform light.

Beams from track lighting with spot bulbs accent these pots and highlight their shapes.

LIGHTING FOR MOOD AND ATMOSPHERE

The basic lighting effects described on pages 10–11 are used to create different moods in a room. Lighting can produce any mood you want.

Lighting in this family room enhances the dramatic dark walls, highlights the paintings, defines social areas, and provides soft ambient light for viewing television.

DRAMATIC

Dramatic lighting uses contrasting highlights and shadows. Small areas of light are often separated by larger, darker ones, as in theatrical lighting. Accent lighting, concentrated beams of light aimed at the objects considered most important in the space, is an effective technique for achieving dramatic lighting effects.

INTIMATE

Glowing pools of light with soft edges—like the low light from table lamps or candles in an elegant restaurant—lend a sense of intimacy. People want to lean toward the glow. You can create an intimate feeling in any room with shaded table and floor lamps, especially at eye level. Beams of light, if not intense, make intimate light pools.

RELAXED

Lighting that washes the walls and ceiling to fill a room evenly creates a relaxed atmosphere. Your eyes move easily around

the room. Nothing is hidden in shadow and there are no bright spots to fight for your attention, unifying the room into a pleasant space. You can achieve a relaxed feeling by using many light sources that overlap to brighten the room.

FORMAL

Symmetrical lighting that has a clear focus along with some highlights imparts a sense of formality. An example is a dining room with a central chandelier and flanking wall fixtures.

FUNCTIONAL

Reading, cooking, and grooming—the most common household tasks—require lighting that spreads evenly over the work. Contrast and shadows make it harder to work. On the other hand, manipulating models or other three-dimensional objects is often easier under a more intense beam of light that penetrates depths and reveals form. If background lighting is not comfortably diffused, the area probably will be tiring to work in. Working with dark materials (such as sewing navy blue fabric) demands more light. Looking at computer and television screens requires relatively little light. You will learn more about lighting for specific tasks and task areas in the room-by-room recommendations on pages 48–73.

Shaded floor lamps cast the easy chairs into pools of light to create intimacy in a large room.

Recessed ceiling lights, floor lamps, and table lamps light this room evenly to give it a relaxing atmosphere.

LIGHTING TECHNIQUES

Lighting techniques involve the selection and placement of lighting equipment to produce a desired effect. Lighting terms are broad and many terms overlap, as you will see. Often terms are combined to arrive at a lighting solution. For example, downlighting a living room with beams of light will reveal the form and texture of the furnishings and create a dramatic mood at the same time.

DOWNLIGHTING

Downlighting directs light down from the ceiling or a hanging fixture to illuminate an object or surface below it, such as a table or countertop. Downlighting is a direct lighting effect. Depending on the type of fixture and layout, downlighting may create concentrated beams of light with strong highlights and shadows that show off the form of objects, or it may illuminate a large area with broader floods of soft, diffused light.

Cove lights above the cabinets in this kitchen brighten the ceiling. Undercabinet lights illuminate the work surface and light the wall to eliminate shadows.

Wall brackets provide task lighting for the kitchen office space above. Downlighting in the alcove at left accents the three pieces of art effectively.

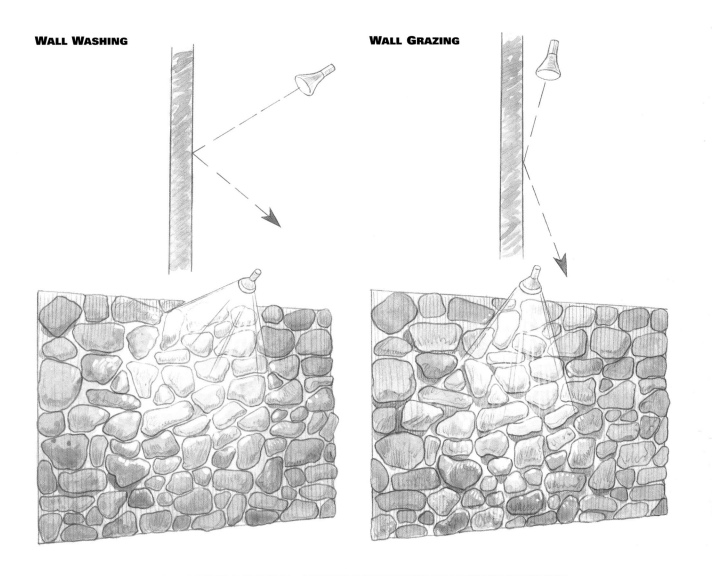

WALL WASHING

WALL GRAZING

UPLIGHTING

Uplighting reflects light off the ceiling for a soft and comfortable indirect lighting effect. Uplighting can originate from hanging fixtures, portable lamps (called torchères), wall fixtures, or built-in cove lights. Uplighting makes the ceiling the brightest plane of the room.

WALL WASHING

A wide beam of light aimed at a wall from a few feet away creates a wash of light. *Wall washing* works best with a relatively even spread of light on the wall so the surface appears as a single luminous plane. Wall washing brightens a space and makes it seem open and generous.

WALL GRAZING

Grazing light rakes a wall at an acute angle from fixtures placed close to a wall. Grazing light creates interesting highlights and shadows on textured surfaces. *Wall grazing* works best on textured surfaces, such as brick, stone, and nubby fabric.

ACCENT LIGHTING

Focused light—*accent lighting*—draws attention to an object or an area and highlights or accents it. *Spotlighting* uses a concentrated beam for the accent. *Floodlighting* uses a defined wash to cover a larger object.

TASK LIGHTING

Light applied for the purpose of viewing or performing a specific task is called *task lighting*. The quality of the light can vary, depending on the nature of the task.

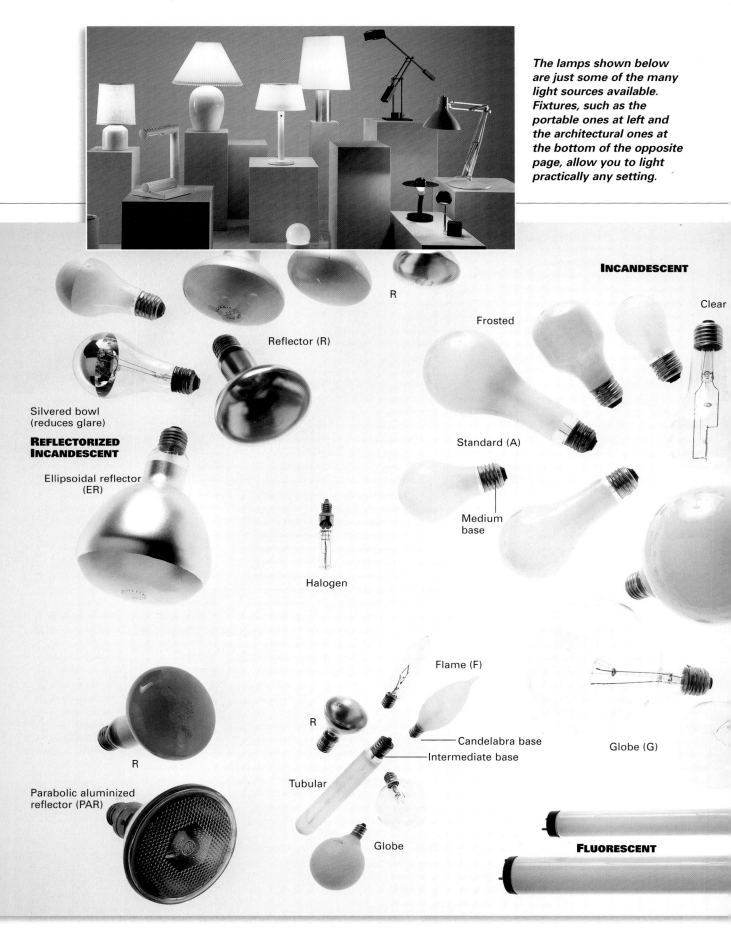

The lamps shown below are just some of the many light sources available. Fixtures, such as the portable ones at left and the architectural ones at the bottom of the opposite page, allow you to light practically any setting.

INCANDESCENT

Clear

Frosted

R

Reflector (R)

Standard (A)

Silvered bowl
(reduces glare)

REFLECTORIZED
INCANDESCENT

Ellipsoidal reflector
(ER)

Medium
base

Halogen

Flame (F)

R

Candelabra base

Globe (G)

Intermediate base

R

Tubular

Parabolic aluminized
reflector (PAR)

Globe

FLUORESCENT

LIGHT SOURCES

Electric light sources are called lamps, but are commonly known as bulbs or tubes, after their glass enclosures. (The lighting devices that sit on tables or stand on floors—commonly known as lamps—are called portables in the industry.)

The three principal electric light technologies are incandescent, fluorescent, and high-intensity discharge (HID). Incandescent bulbs are the most popular residential light source. Fluorescent sources are common in commercial and institutional lighting. HID sources are most often found in industrial buildings, gymnasiums, and in outdoor lighting of all types. Daylight is an important source but, due to its inherent variability, seldom serves as the primary source of indoor illumination.

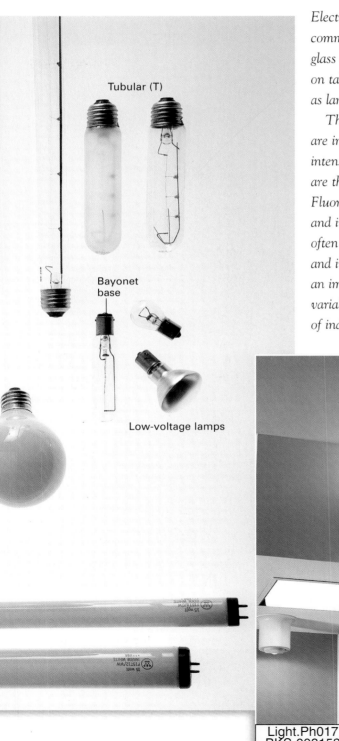

Tubular (T)

Bayonet base

Low-voltage lamps

Light.Ph017
BKS 008153

LIGHT OUTPUT

Light output is measured in lumens. The output of most incandescent bulbs (and some fluorescent replacements) is printed on their packaging. You also can find lumen ratings in lamp manufacturers' catalogs (printed or on the Internet). Small incandescent bulbs in a chandelier may emit only 100 lumens each; a fluorescent tube can produce more than 3,000 lumens.

The electrical power consumed by a lightbulb is measured in watts (W). The watt rating is marked on most bulbs. While the power of a light source is often expressed in watts (a 60-watt bulb, for example), using wattage to compare lighting power is only valid when comparing light sources that are the same type.

How efficiently a light source converts power into light is expressed in lumens per watt (LPW). There's a wide range in efficiency: The least efficient incandescent bulbs used in homes produce about 5 LPW; the most efficient fluorescent lamps produce more than 90 LPW.

For any type of lamp, physically larger bulbs generally produce more light than smaller ones. However the same is not true when comparing lamps of different types. Sometimes a smaller lamp of one type (a halogen bulb, for instance) produces more light than a larger one of a different type (a standard incandescent bulb, for instance). And the same size and type of incandescent lamp is often available in two or more different wattages and lumen outputs. Although this can be confusing, it offers flexibility in achieving the desired lighting effect from a particular fixture.

LAMP LIFE

As with light output, the rated life of incandescent lightbulbs (in hours) appears on their packaging. The number is an average, based on a large sample of lamps tested in a laboratory. The rated life is the point at which half of the test sample has failed and half is still operating. (This is a conservative measurement that discounts the effect of the few lamps that last a very long time.) The actual life of any bulb in use varies; some last longer than the rated life and some fail sooner. Extreme temperatures or vibration can shorten a bulb's life. And a lightbulb that fails before half of its rated life may mean there's a problem with a lighting fixture or the wiring.

Most incandescent bulbs have a rated life of 750–3,000 hours. Fluorescent lamps are rated to last 10,000–20,000 hours. (A bulb that's lit for eight hours per day is on for 2,920 hours per year; one that's lit 24 hours a day is on for 8,760 hours per year.)

Incandescent lamps operate efficiently in a wide range of ambient temperatures

Daylight accurately shows all the colors in the room above. Incandescent lighting reveals the colors differently, below. Incandescent light has a different balance of red, yellow, and orange than daylight, so many colors appear warmer.

so they are suitable for either indoor or outdoor use. Fluorescent sources perform poorly in abnormally hot or cold environments, so they are less practical for outdoor lighting.

THE COLOR OF LIGHT

White light varies in its appearance and its ability to render colors naturally. Color appearance is often described by such terms as *warm* and *cool*. Color temperature is a measure of the color appearance of a light source. The ability of a light source to show colors accurately is measured by its Color Rendering Index (CRI). Most incandescent sources appear relatively warm and render colors well. Lamps with the element neodymium in the glass have a blue tint to help them render colors more accurately. Fluorescent sources exhibit a wide range of performance. A source with a CRI of 100 shows colors perfectly; lower numbers indicate less accurate color rendition.

COLOR TEMPERATURE CHART

COLOR TEMPERATURE	MOOD OR FEELING	COLOR OF LIGHT	EXAMPLES
1800K	VERY WARM	RED-YELLOW	Candle flame Sodium lamps Sunset (clear sky) First Sunrise
2800K	WARM	RED-YELLOW-WHITE	Incandescent lamps Sunlight, 25 minutes before setting (clear sky)
3500K	INTERMEDIATE	SLIGHTLY REDDISH WHITE	Film studio lamps Sunlight, 45 minutes before setting (clear sky)
4100K	COOL	NEUTRAL WHITE	Cool fluorescent lamps Sunlight, 60 minutes before setting (clear sky)
5000K	COLD	SLIGHTLY BLUISH WHITE	Sun overhead (summer, clear sky)
7500K	ICY	VERY BLUISH WHITE	Cloudy winter daylight

LIGHTBULB TERMINOLOGY

Bulbs are classified by wattage, shape, and diameter (expressed in eighths of an inch). So a 60A19 bulb is a 60-watt, style-A bulb (the standard bulb shape) that is 2⅜ (¹⁹⁄₈) inches in diameter at its widest point. This basic terminology does not reveal either the lumen output or the lamp life; you need to look up that information.

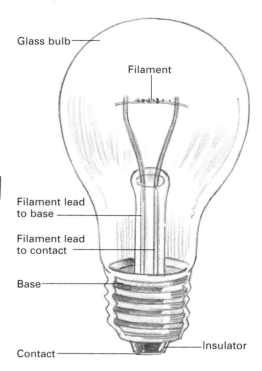

Glass bulb
Filament
Filament lead to base
Filament lead to contact
Base
Contact
Insulator

INCANDESCENT LAMPS

An incandescent lamp generates light by heating a thin filament wire until it glows, or incandesces. Incandescent sources produce a warm, yellowish light that most people think is pleasant and familiar. Incandescent sources are available in a wide range of sizes (allowing creativity in the use of lighting equipment) and are easily dimmed. They are relatively inefficient in converting electrical power into light, however, and usually don't last very long. These drawbacks can make them costly and inconvenient to use.

INCANDESCENT BULBS

Type A

Type F

Halogen (T4)

Reflectorized halogen (Type MR)

Type T

Reflectorized (Type PAR)

Type G

NONREFLECTORIZED INCANDESCENT LAMPS

Nonreflectorized bulbs emit light in all directions. The most common type is the A lamp, used in many portables, enclosed ceiling and wall fixtures, and some recessed downlights. Other common shapes include G (globe) bulbs, used in many bathroom and decorative lighting fixtures; F (flame) bulbs, often used in chandeliers; and T (tubular) bulbs, used in chandeliers, wall brackets, portable lamps, range hoods, and specialty lamps.

Standard A bulbs are available from 25 to 250 watts in four types.

■ **FROSTED:** The glass of a frosted bulb is etched to diffuse the light. A soft white bulb diffuses the light more, making it good for use as a reading lamp.

■ **CLEAR:** Clear bulbs emit bright but harsh light.

■ **THREE-WAY:** The two filaments in a three-way bulb produce three levels of brightness when turned on separately or together.

■ **LONG-LIFE:** The thicker filament in these bulbs does not burn out as fast, but you lose some light output for the longer life (typically one-third more hours).

REFLECTORIZED LAMPS

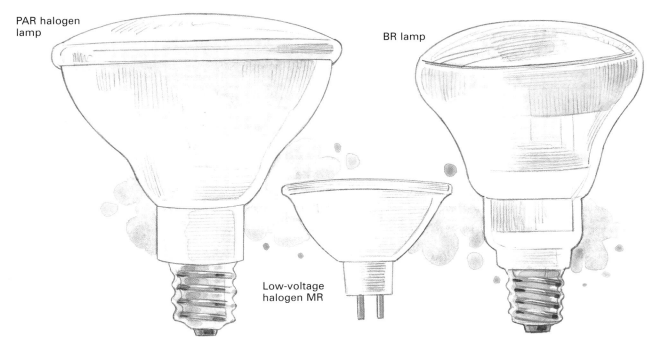

PAR halogen lamp

BR lamp

Low-voltage halogen MR

Incandescent lamps described as *energy-saving* bulbs usually operate at a lower wattage and put out less light than similar incandescent bulbs, with little real difference in efficiency. In some cases the energy-saving label may refer to a more efficient technology. A knowledgeable dealer or careful reading of the product packaging can help you determine which bulbs give the most light per watt consumed.

REFLECTORIZED INCANDESCENT LAMPS

Reflectorized lamps create a beam of light. A concentrated beam is known as a *spot*; a broader beam is a *flood*. The type of reflector built into the lamp gives it a sharp edge or one that feathers out.

■ **R OR BR:** These lamps emit a smooth field of light with a soft edge. They are commonly used in recessed downlights.

■ **PAR:** Often installed for accent lighting or for direct lighting from a distance, these lamps produce a hot spot in the center of the beam and a hard edge.

■ **MR:** These are among the smallest reflectorized lamps and produce beams similar to PAR lamps. They use low-voltage technology to achieve their compact size. (See "Low-Voltage Lamps," *right*.)

Designations for reflectorized lamps are similar to those for other types of incandescent lamps: 50PAR30SP is a 50-watt PAR lamp that is 3¾ (³⁰⁄₈) inches in diameter and produces a spot beam; FL is a flood beam.

LOW-VOLTAGE LAMPS

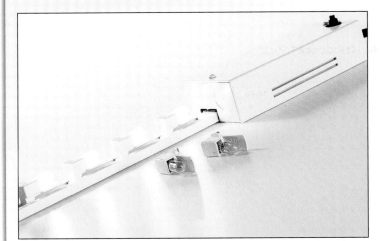

Electrical circuits in American homes operate at 110–120 volts. Most incandescent lightbulbs operate directly from these circuits and are called line-voltage lamps. Lamps that operate on lower voltage can be smaller than line-voltage bulbs. This permits small lighting fixtures and—with reflectorized bulbs—a more precise beam of light. Lights that operate at reduced voltage are called low-voltage lamps.

Low-voltage light sources require a transformer, which reduces the electrical voltage to the correct level for the lamp. (Most operate at 12 volts.) When the transformer mounts in the fixture itself—typical for track lights and recessed downlights—the fixture receives line voltage, but the lamp itself receives the low voltage. When the transformer is a separate unit (as in most landscape lighting systems), low voltage is supplied to the light fixture. The transformer, fixtures, and connecting wires for such an installation are called a low-voltage system.

LIGHTBULB TERMINOLOGY
continued

HALOGEN AND XENON LAMPS

Halogen and Xenon lamps are incandescent light sources. Halogen bulbs contain bromine and iodine that help redeposit tungsten onto the filament as it burns off. That's why the filament can operate at a higher temperature without burning out and why the bulb produces whiter light than an ordinary incandescent bulb. It's also more efficient. Halogen bulbs can be small, so they work well in low-voltage applications. Low-voltage MR lamps are halogen, as are line-voltage PAR lamps. Another popular halogen bulb is the higher wattage T lamp, often used in torchères and some wall fixtures.

Xenon lamps have become popular in low-voltage fixtures and systems used for under-cabinet and cove lighting. They offer long life but aren't as efficient as halogen bulbs, and their light is not as white.

FLUORESCENT LAMPS

Current passing through mercury vapor in a fluorescent bulb makes ultraviolet light that causes the phosphor coating on the inside of the tube to fluoresce, or glow, producing visible light. Compared with incandescent light sources, fluorescent lamps are three to five times as efficient and five to 20 times as long-lasting. In residential lighting they are most useful where a lot of light is needed,

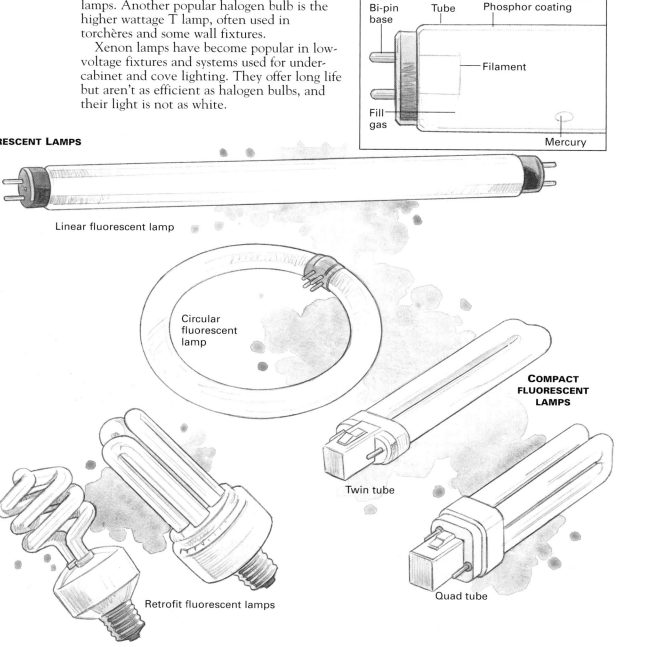

FLUORESCENT LAMPS

Linear fluorescent lamp

Circular fluorescent lamp

Retrofit fluorescent lamps

COMPACT FLUORESCENT LAMPS

Twin tube

Quad tube

Bi-pin base · Tube · Phosphor coating · Filament · Fill gas · Mercury as in a kitchen, home office, utility room, or workshop. High efficiency and long life make them useful where lights operate for long periods, as in a hallway or rear entry. Because of their size and shape, they create a broadly dispersed spread of light.

Linear fluorescent lamps come in many standard diameters and lengths. Longer tubes usually produce more light. Linear fluorescent tubes distribute light equally along their length and are effective for lighting a large area, such as a countertop or worktable. Designations for linear fluorescent lamps are similar to those for incandescent lamps. For example, F32T8 means a fluorescent tube that uses 32 watts and is 1 (⅛) inch in diameter. The length and light output of the tube (in this case 48 inches and 2,800 lumens) are not part of the lamp description; you can find that information on the package or in a catalog.

The tube of a compact fluorescent lamp (often abbreviated as CFL) is bent to minimize the lamp's bulk. Common compact fluorescent lamps are often described as twin tube, quad tube, triple tube, and so forth. Compact fluorescent lamps are most easily described by their shape and wattage (32-watt, triple tube, for example).

THE COLOR OF FLUORESCENT LIGHT

Fluorescent light color depends on the phosphors that make up the tube coating. The color can appear relatively warm, like an incandescent lamp, or cool, but not as cool as daylight. If the phosphors are of good quality, fluorescent light can render colors accurately. Remember that your ability to see colors depends on the color in the light.

A fluorescent lamp for residential use should make a warm light and render colors well. The most appropriate lamp for residential use carries the technical suffix 830 at the end of the lamp designation. (For example, F32T8/830.) Many manufacturers use trade names to identify lamps that are warm or render colors well.

HID LAMPS

High-intensity discharge (HID) lamps produce light when an electric current stimulates chemical compounds inside the bulb. HID sources are named for the chemicals they contain. Sodium lamps are found in many street and security lights. Metal halide lamps are used in athletic facilities and some stores. Mercury lamps—

the oldest and least efficient—are often used in landscape applications.

Despite their high efficiency and long life, HID sources do not usually work well for home lighting. They produce too much light—often of poor color quality—and many have bulky and expensive electrical apparatus. An exception is in outdoor lighting, where compact HID lamps are effective for floodlighting driveways and large trees.

EMERGING LIGHT SOURCES

For most of history, flames from wood, pitch, or oil illuminated homes. Electric lighting is about 100 years old. While both incandescent and fluorescent sources continually improve, new sources are emerging. Light-emitting diodes (LEDs), now widely used in automotive lighting, are beginning to be used in commercial lighting as well. LEDs are small, long-lasting, and relatively efficient sources that work well for concealed lighting. Manufacturers are rapidly reducing the high cost and improving the cool color of LEDs, suggesting they might be suitable for a wider array of lighting uses in the future. Induction lamps—a form of fluorescent lighting—can operate in any temperature for as long as 20 years without replacement. They could become the outdoor and street lighting of the future.

FLUORESCENT BALLASTS

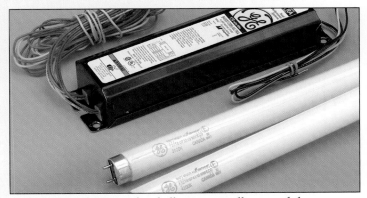

A fluorescent lamp needs a ballast—generally part of the fixture—to work properly. The best ballasts are based on electronic technology that eliminates the annoying hum and flicker that most people find objectionable. Some compact fluorescent lamps have a ballast in the base and can replace incandescent Type A lamps where they will fit physically. These self-ballasted lamps—shown on the opposite page—are called *retrofit, screw-in,* or *replacement* CFLs.

LIGHTING FIXTURES

origins—chandelier or sconce, for example. Others are named for the lighting effects they produce, such as downlight or accent light, for example. Still others are simply described by how they mount in the space—recessed, pendant or wall bracket. Some fixtures are described by the light source—fluorescent, for example—but that is too broad a category to help in selection.

Lighting fixtures are usually made up of a housing that holds all components and mounts to a structure, a socket (or sockets) to hold the lamp or lamps, and optics that control the light. Optics may be reflectors, diffusers, lenses, or refractive crystals.

Fixtures are divided into three categories: decorative, architectural, and outdoor.

A lighting fixture holds and controls the light source, mounts to the structure, and connects to the electrical wiring. Some fixtures carry distinctive names that are usually derived from their pre-electricity

DECORATIVE LIGHTING

Decorative fixtures are completely visible; their size, form, and style all contribute to the decor of the home. Decorative lighting fixtures mount on a separate junction box installed in the ceiling or wall.

CHANDELIERS AND PENDANTS:
Chandeliers and pendants hang from the ceiling on a chain, cable, rod, or cord. Distinctive chandeliers are usually the featured lighting fixture in dining rooms and entries. Small ones are used over tables and counters, often for task lighting.

A chandelier—the style evolved from hanging candle holders—typically consists

PENDANTS

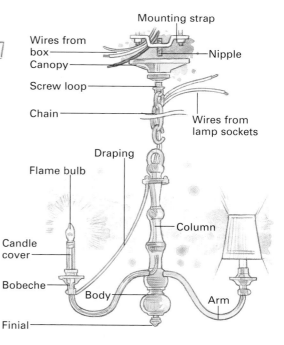

of several arms with individual lights. Exposed bulbs help create a festive and formal glitter. With shaded bulbs, the effect is an attractive glow that draws attention. Large indirect pendants with glass diffusers create a comfortable and relaxing wash of uplight.

Downlight pendants use a metal shade to reflect light down onto a surface, offering effective task light for homework or general reading. Miniature pendants often have glow-glass diffusers, sometimes in dramatic colors. They can be grouped attractively over an open counter or buffet.

Chandeliers and pendants are usually described by their diameter (in inches), as well as by the number of bulbs, materials, style, and finish. You can adjust the length of the hanging chain or cord, but solid-rod or tube suspensions are often of standard fixed lengths.

WALL FIXTURES: Wall fixtures, also called brackets, are available in several forms. A sconce (named for a covered candle holder) can sparkle with an exposed bulb or glow with a glass or translucent diffuser. Wall fixtures that coordinate with a chandelier of the same style lend a formal air to a room.

An urn or uplight bracket directs light toward the ceiling for an indirect lighting effect. Elongated wall brackets serve as grooming lights over mirrors and are also known as bath brackets. Because indirect and bath brackets distribute light over a larger area, they can accept more—or higher-output—lightbulbs. Smaller wall brackets look harsh if they are too bright. Where you can look down into a wall fixture from a stairway or balcony, install an enclosed one so it won't glare.

Wall brackets are usually described by their size—length, width, and projection from the wall—as well as the specific light source, materials, style, and finish.

CEILING FIXTURES: Fixtures that mount directly against the ceiling are sometimes called flush-mounts. They direct most of the light into the room, with a small spill of light onto the ceiling around the fixture. Fixtures that hang down several inches on short rods or chain are called close-to-ceiling fixtures. They distribute light up onto the ceiling, as well as down into the room. This brightens the space and softens the contrast between the lighted fixture and the darker ceiling.

Small ceiling-mounted fixtures (those less than 20 inches in diameter) usually use A shape incandescent lamps or compact fluorescent lamps. They are particularly useful in hallways, closets, pantries, and other small rooms. Larger rectangular fixtures usually use linear fluorescent lamps and can provide a substantial amount of light, which is helpful

WALL FIXTURES

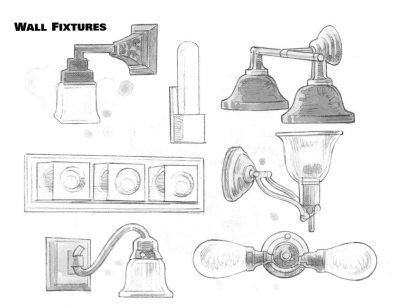

CEILING FIXTURES

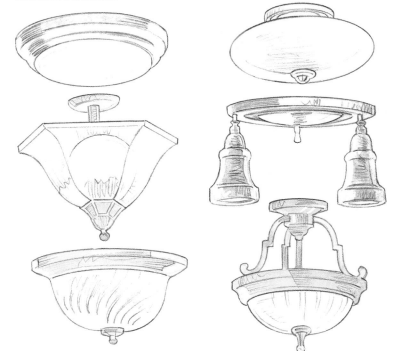

in a kitchen or work area. (A single 24×48-inch fixture with four fluorescent tubes produces more light than four incandescent fixtures with three 60-watt bulbs each.)

Decorative ceiling fixtures, styled to match chandeliers, are often used in foyers with low ceilings. More utilitarian designs are better for hallways or a rear entry.

Lamps on most ceiling fixtures are completely enclosed by a glass or plastic diffuser. You change the lightbulbs by twisting off the diffuser, pulling it down on captive spring retainers, or by removing thumbscrews.

LIGHTING FIXTURES
continued

PORTABLES: Decorative fixtures not attached to the walls or ceiling—often called table lamps or floor lamps—are known in the industry as portables. They come in a wide range of styles, from strictly utilitarian to elaborate artistic creations.

LIGHTING STYLES: Many lighting fixtures derive their style from the 17th through 19th centuries. Modern style lighting owes its clean lines and geometric forms to 20th-century design. Contemporary styles reflect current design ideas and often blend traditional forms and modern materials or vice versa. Decorative fixtures said to be architectural in style emphasize machine-made rather than handcrafted components.

TABLE LAMPS

READING LAMPS

ARCHITECTURAL LIGHTING

Architectural lighting refers to track lighting and lighting built into the architecture of the home, such as recessed downlights, cove lights, pockets and valances, or concealed task lighting. Concealed architectural lighting, such as recessed downlights and coves, lights a space without visible lighting equipment. The light, rather than the fixture, becomes the focus of attention.

Unlike decorative lighting fixtures, which are usually used individually around the room, architectural lighting equipment is most often organized into groups or systems.

RECESSED DOWNLIGHTS: Recessed downlights, also called *downlights*, *high hats*, or *cans*, are installed above the ceiling and shine into the room through a hole in the ceiling.

Downlights, originally theatrical lighting, were first widely used in commercial and civic architecture in the 1950s. They later found their way into custom homes and became popular for home lighting in the 1980s.

Downlights consist of a frame and a trim, usually purchased separately. The frame (or housing) installs between the ceiling joists. Connections to the house wiring are made inside a junction box attached to the frame.

The trim gives the installation a finished look and contains the optics that create the desired light effect. It is held by springs or clips on the frame.

Downlight frames are available in many styles within three basic categories:

■ Frames rated for insulation contact (IC) may be completely buried in thermal insulation or surrounded by it, as is typical in the top floor of a home. Thermal insulation must be kept at least 3 inches from a non-IC downlight.

■ New-construction frames are installed when the joists are still accessible—before the ceiling is enclosed—when framing a new home or during remodeling or renovation.

■ Remodeler frames can be installed in an existing ceiling. They are used when there is no access above the ceiling. (See "Installing Recessed Downlights" on page 96.)

Most frames accept incandescent A, R, and PAR lamps. Special frames are required for most low-voltage MR lamps and compact fluorescent lamps.

DOWNLIGHT TRIM: Downlight trim gives the installation a finished look and, with the light source, determines the lighting effect. Trims are usually described by appearance or material instead of their light effect:

■ Open trim is a simple ring that covers the ceiling cutout; it is inexpensive but glary.

■ Baffled trim includes a ridged cylinder that absorbs stray light, reducing glare.

■ Reflector trim concentrates light into a beam and directs it away from people's eyes. Reflectors are the most efficient and usually the most comfortable downlights.

The three types above are good for general or ambient lighting in kitchens, dining areas, living rooms, bedrooms, and hallways. With narrow-beam reflectorized lamps, they produce a concentrated beam of light. Flood bulbs, A-shape lamps, or compact fluorescent lamps will make a wider beam.

■ Enclosed downlights with lenses shield the bulb with a glass or plastic diffuser. When gaskets are used to keep out moisture, these work well in showers and bathrooms. Because the diffuser wipes clean easily, enclosed downlights are sometimes recommended over a sink or range.

■ Wall-washer trims have reflectors or lenses that direct light onto a wall—both up and down and side to side. Wall washers are most effective when used in groups of two or more, spread along the wall.

■ Accent lights create a beam that can highlight art or other objects. You can aim the beam from the reflectorized bulb by adjusting the bracket that holds the socket inside the frame. Eyeballs—which protrude down from the ceiling—and pinholes—which are enclosed by a flat plate—are two popular types of accent lights.

COVE LIGHTS: Cove lighting—a linear light source concealed behind a fascia on the wall or on top of cabinets—creates an indirect lighting effect when it reflects off the ceiling. The same lighting system can be used behind a cornice at the top of a wall to cast light down the wall into the room. When used behind a valance mounted on the wall or under cabinets near eye level, the light is both direct and indirect.

Fluorescent strip lights are the best fixtures for providing bright, widespread light from a cove. A strip light has one or two fluorescent tubes mounted on a base that contains the ballast. The strips are wired together and either butted end to end or overlapped by 3 to 6 inches in order to create a continuous line of light. The cove must be large enough that it will not trap the light. Fluorescent cove lighting works best in kitchens and other workspaces. Similar fixtures installed under kitchen cabinets provide task lighting.

RECESSED DOWNLIGHTS

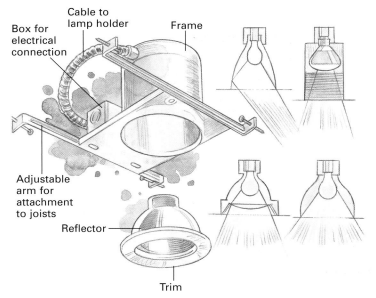

Box for electrical connection · Cable to lamp holder · Frame · Adjustable arm for attachment to joists · Reflector · Trim

A low-voltage system can create a soft wash of light that accents the ceiling. The system includes a continuous wire way— or track—and small, low-voltage lighting elements that attach to it. A remote transformer, usually concealed nearby, provides the low-voltage electrical supply to the system. The transformer is sized to the length of the track and the number and wattage of the lights. Low-voltage coves work well in dining rooms, living rooms, bedrooms, and entries—spaces that do not need a lot of light from the cove.

Rope light—a flexible plastic tube containing tiny incandescent bulbs—makes a subtle line of light around the bottom of a cabinet or in a small cove. The strand is easy to cut to length and fits into a narrow space.

UNDERCABINET LIGHTING

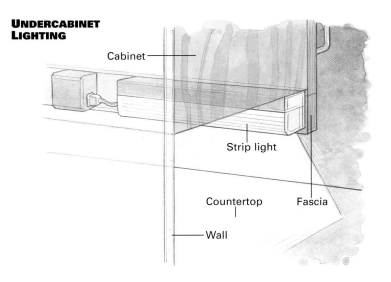

Cabinet · Strip light · Countertop · Fascia · Wall

LIGHTING FIXTURES
continued

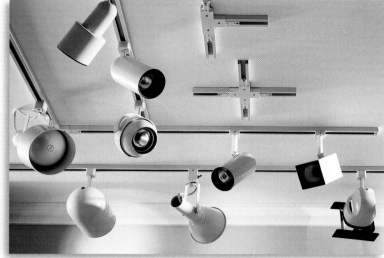

Flexible and adaptable track lighting works well in many lighting situations.

TRACK LIGHTING: Track lighting, invented in the 1960s, offers the greatest flexibility in locating and aiming accent light. Widely used in stores and museums, it also works well in homes for lighting art and collectibles. Also, the flexibility of the track system permits you to bring light anywhere in the home, even if there isn't a convenient outlet.

Track lighting consists of an electrified track and movable track lights—usually adjustable—that attach to it. The electrified track is a metal channel, U- or H-shape, in sections, enclosing insulated electrical conductors. The track is sold in sections 2–12 feet long that can be installed individually, cut to length, plugged together to form long runs, or joined with corner connectors to form patterns. You can power the track at either end (a live end) or anywhere along its length (a floating feed). You can install track on the ceiling or on a wall, either on the surface or recessed flush. Or the track can stand off from the mounting surface on stems.

Each track light has an adapter base that holds the fixture to the track and makes the electrical connection. Track lights can be positioned or repositioned at any point on the track and aimed as desired.

Track lights themselves are essentially sockets enclosed in fixed or articulated housings that hold the lamp. Some track lights accept only a particular type of lamp, but others take several kinds so you can choose the lamp according to its size, intensity, and beam spread in order to create the desired effect. Different types of track lights incorporate shades, cowls, shrouds, or louvers to block stray light and create a comfortable and glare-free beam.

A low-voltage track light set includes a transformer, uses a low-voltage lamp, and connects to standard track (and can be used with line voltage track lights). On the other hand, a low-voltage track system uses a remote transformer to power the entire track. A low-voltage system uses only low-voltage lamp holders without transformers. These are the smallest track fixtures available, creating a distinctively miniaturized lighting installation. Many low-voltage systems use nonreflectorized low-voltage bulbs in decorative shades. Suspended on small stems, they create a free-form decorative chandelier.

Lighting track, either standard or low-voltage, can also hold decorative pendants fitted with the appropriate adapters.

TRACK LIGHTING

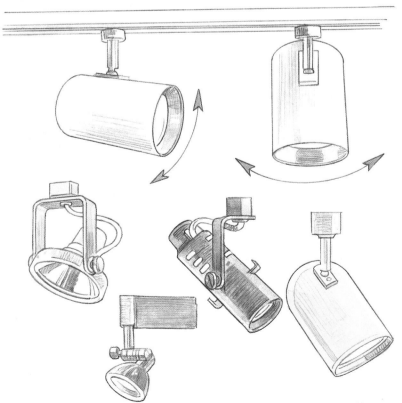

OUTDOOR LIGHTING

Outdoor lighting equipment faces several distinctive challenges: It must be able to withstand the weather, it must have suitable mountings and electrical connections, and it must provide effective light. So, while some outdoor lighting fixtures can be used indoors, most indoor equipment cannot be used outside. Fixtures approved for use in an outdoor overhang (a recessed downlight, for example) will be labeled for use in damp locations; fixtures to be installed anywhere else outside must be approved for use in wet locations. Incandescent and HID light sources operate in most outdoor temperatures. Fluorescent lamps, however, are sensitive to temperature and will have problems with starting and light output in cold weather.

ENTRY LIGHTING: Lanterns enclosed by clear or decorated glass panels can hang over a doorway or mount to the wall on either side. Other solutions include fully enclosed marine-style wall brackets, diffusing globes, utility-style fixtures, and bracket-mounted cylinders. Post-top versions of entry lights can be used at the beginning of a driveway, provided that electrical service is available there. Step lights mount in the wall a foot or two above the step, and direct light across the tread. Step lights can also be used indoors.

SECURITY AND FLOODLIGHTING: Simple PAR lamp holders that have sockets with gaskets provide an easy way to illuminate exterior grounds from the exterior of the home, but they may glare. High-wattage halogen flood lights provide a wider beam and better coverage of pavement. HID wallpacks and post- or wall-mounted dusk-to-dawn refractors offer even more light and longer life. But their industrial appearance may be inappropriate for some homes.

LANDSCAPE LIGHTING:
Landscape lighting refers generally to fixtures installed in gardens and around trees, pathways, patios, or gardens. Most landscape lighting equipment runs on a low-voltage system. A remote transformer, plugged into an exterior outlet, supplies 12 volts of power to weatherproof cable. You splice the low-voltage lighting elements onto the cable wherever you want, then stake them into the ground (or onto a tree). The number and wattage of the lighting elements determines the size of the transformer and the maximum length of the cable. (See page 83 for voltage drop guidelines.)

The pierced reflector on this path light adds sparkle.

Path or spread lights support a reflector or shade and mount on top of a short pole. They create a pool of light on the ground. When the lights are spaced close together, the pools form a continuous path or spread of light. Deck lights mount to railings or walls, where they can shine onto the patio surface or onto steps.

Accent lights enclose reflectorized bulbs in a hood or cowl that blocks the view of the bright light source (which would be especially irritating at night). Aimed up at the canopy of a tree or at shrubbery and statues, the beam from an accent fixture highlights features in the landscape or garden. Floodlights direct the light from nonreflectorized bulbs onto larger surfaces, such as a stone wall.

ENTRY LIGHTING

LANDSCAPE LIGHTING

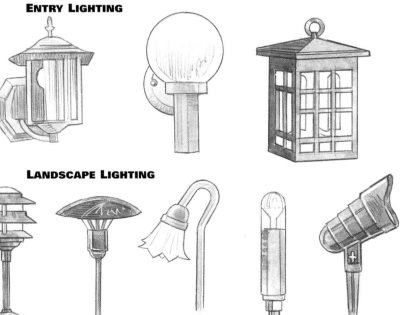

LIGHTING CONTROLS

The National Electric Code (NEC) requires a lighting control at the entry to every room. The control can be a switch or a dimmer, or a remote control linked to a central lighting control system.

Switches turn lights on and off to provide a single level of illumination. Dimmers adjust lighting intensity so you can select the level that best fits an activity, mood, or personal preference. Semiconductor and digital electronic technologies have dramatically enhanced the versatility and performance of lighting controls while reducing their cost.

Separate controls for each layer of lighting let you adjust the atmosphere of a room to suit any occasion.

SWITCHES

A single-pole switch turns lights on and off from one location. A pair of three-way switches can be wired together to control lights from two locations (at either end of a hall or stairway, for example). An additional wire—called a *traveler*—is used in the circuit. Although they are called three-way switches, only two are used together. Adding a four-way switch between the three-way switches in a circuit allows you to control one fixture from three points.

DIMMERS

Simple dimmer   Preset dimmer   Digital dimmer

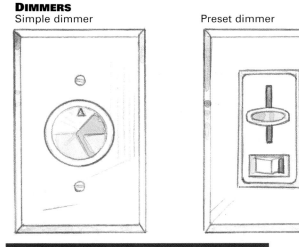 

DIMMING

Theaters used light dimmers before most homes even had electric lights. Those early resistance-type dimmers simply added more resistance to the light's electrical circuit, reducing the power to the bulb. The excess energy turned into waste heat; the lights dimmed, but no energy was saved. In a modern dimmer, a solid-state electronic switch called a triac turns the electricity to a light on and off 120 times per second. The length of time (in thousandths of a second) that the current flow remains off determines how dim the light will be. The internal switching occurs so rapidly that it is usually imperceptible. By completely turning off the electricity to the bulb for a time, dimmers save energy as they reduce light output.

Dimming extends the life of incandescent bulbs—often significantly. Dimming a lamp by 10 percent doubles its life; dimming it by 25 percent will extend lamp life by four times. Where changing a lightbulb is difficult— in a tall entry, for example—dim the lamp to prolong its life.

There are three types of dimmers available: **SIMPLE DIMMER:** A simple dimmer turns on when you begin to increase the intensity; it turns off after you have reached the lowest light level. Every time you turn on the lights with a simple dimmer you must reset the intensity. Simple dimmers offer a choice of rotary knob, slider, or toggle control. All simple dimmers are single-pole devices. They control lights from one location in the room and cannot be wired to any other control.

PRESET DIMMER: A preset dimmer has separate on/off and intensity controls. You set the intensity to the level you want and turn the lights on to that level (called the *preset*). Of course you can change the intensity at any time by adjusting the dimming control (which creates a new preset). A preset rotary dimmer turns on and off when you push the knob in (also called a *push-push dimmer*).

A preset slider includes a rocker or press switch. A preset toggle dimmer uses the toggle for on/off control and adds a small lever to adjust the intensity. A three-way preset dimmer can be wired with a three-way or remote switch to provide two control locations in the room. The three-way switch turns the lights on and off; only the dimmer can adjust the intensity.

DIGITAL DIMMER: A digital dimmer has a microchip processor, which augments its capabilities beyond that of a conventional preset dimmer. You adjust the intensity at any time by pressing a paddle control until the light reaches the desired level. The digital dimmer memorizes two presets—one you can set and another for full brightness. Tap the top of the paddle once and the dimmer turns on to your preset; tap it a second time, and the dimmer goes to full brightness. Tap the bottom of the paddle and the dimmer fades off. Programming the preset is simple: Adjust the lights to the level you want and push a set button. You can change the intensity at any time, which overrides your custom preset, but does not erase it. This is convenient if you just want to raise or lower the light level temporarily.

Digital dimmers can be wired together to provide multiple points of control around a room; any dimmer can change the intensity, as well as turn lights on and off.

SELECTING A DIMMER: A dimmer must be compatible with the lamp it controls (called the *load*). Incandescent dimmers handle only line-voltage bulbs. Magnetic low-voltage dimmers control low-voltage lamps powered by magnetic transformers. Electronic low-voltage dimmers control low-voltage lamps with electronic transformers. A fluorescent dimmer requires an electronic dimming ballast. These specialized dimmers can also handle line-voltage lamps. (See page 106 for instructions for wiring a dimmer.)

LIGHTING CONTROLS
continued

Central controls allow you to set room lighting from one location. Many controllers have memory settings so you can quickly set favorite lighting schemes.

CENTRAL CONTROLS

Central, or whole-house, controls link lights in different rooms to a central control device, offering added convenience and security. From your bedroom or entry, you can turn on or off all (or some) of the lights in the house and monitor which lights are on. You can operate the lights from a remote control in your car or from farther away through your telephone. And you can link the lighting controls with a security system.

Central control systems can be simple or complex, depending on your needs and the technology you install. For any system, lights in each room are first wired to a compatible control which, in turn, links to a central processor. The difference between systems lies in the link between the light controls and the central processor.

■ A power line carrier (PLC) system—the simplest kind—sends signals through existing electrical wiring; no special cable is needed. PLC-compatible switches, dimmers, and receptacles are installed to control the lights. Signals to and from the central controller travel along the standard electrical power lines. Because no additional wiring is needed, PLC systems can be retrofitted easily. Because control signals for the lighting system travel through the power lines along with electricity for appliances in the home, the system requires careful filtering to ensure consistently clear signals.

■ Dedicated carrier systems link switches, dimmers, and receptacles to the central control with single-purpose wires. The wiring that connects the controls to the central processor is easier to install during new construction, but cables can be pulled through finished walls for retrofit installations. Dedicated carrier systems are the most reliable. Equipment is less expensive than for other systems (depending on complexity), but installation in existing construction can be costly. Some systems interface with a personal computer; others form part of a whole-house electrical control protocol. The more elaborate the system, the more costly it will be.

■ Wireless systems link controls through radio signals. Compatible switches, dimmers, and receptacles receive signals from the

DIMMING SYSTEMS

Several dimmers that are electronically linked to one another make up a dimming system. The system allows control of all lights in a room without adjusting several dimmers separately. These systems are often referred to as *multiscene* dimmers because different levels can be set and saved for each lamp to create a variety of lighting mixes—or scenes—in a room. A dining room might have four scenes: one for formal dining, one for an informal meal, one for homework, and one for cleanup. In each case, the lighting would be different. A dimming system lets you adjust the lights to any of the four scenes by simply pressing a button.

A system of three to six dimmers will fit into a single large-size wall switch box. Or, a number of individual system dimmers in separate locations can be networked together. In either case, most dimming systems include a programming function that lets you store settings that tell the system how you want to light different scenes. You can then call up the different scenes using a pushbutton keypad. Remote keypads let you control the light from anywhere in the room.

control keypads. Repeater stations may be necessary to boost the signal around the house. Wireless systems offer the same flexibility as PLC systems, but they are more expensive. They are relatively easy to install.

SENSORS AND TIMERS

Infrared and ultrasonic motion sensors turn lights on when they detect movement and turn them off after the movement has stopped for a fixed length of time. A passive infrared sensor requires an unobstructed line of sight to its target area so it can detect thermal images. An ultrasonic detector transmits an inaudible sound signal and receives the reflected signals back, detecting motion through shifts in the reflected sound. Motion sensors are often used outdoors to control security lighting. A motion sensor combined with a manual switch is a good control where lights are often left on inadvertently or for places you're likely to enter with your hands full—a basement or attic storage area, for example. With a manual switch, you can override the motion sensor when you want the light to remain on.

Photocell sensors turn lights on when they no longer detect daylight and turn them off when the daylight returns. Porch lights and other exterior lighting often have photocell controls.

Clock timers turn lights on and off at preset times. Timers are often used to turn on landscape lighting or other lights during the evening, then turn them off overnight. Another type of timer switch allows you to turn on a light for a particular length of time. This type is often installed for a bathroom heat lamp.

CENTRAL LIGHTING CONTROLS SCHEMATIC

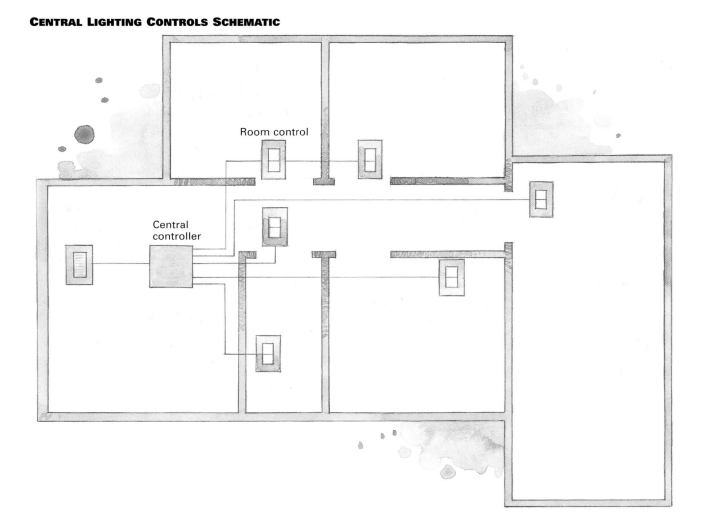

Room control

Central controller

WORKING WITH A DESIGNER

You can light your own home following the advice in this book, but many people can assist you. Knowledgeable salespeople at lighting stores offer a wealth of experience and information. Anyone designated as a "certified lighting consultant" by the American Lighting Association (the trade association for the residential lighting industry) has passed both an objective knowledge-based exam and a complex design project with peer review. Many of them have backgrounds in interior design.

Lighting dealers differ in their approach to design services. Most will advise you informally as part of their normal customer service. A salesperson should be able to provide accurate specifications for all the required parts of lighting products, including those with many components, such as landscape lighting and low-voltage systems. If you want help in creating a lighting plan for your home, however, you may have to pay a fee for the time involved. Such fees are often refundable with your purchase.

You can hire an independent lighting designer to develop a complete plan too. Most designers charge a fee—fixed or hourly—for their services. Some will purchase the equipment they specify for you and charge a commission as compensation for their time. Some lighting designers have formal education in lighting; others have learned through practice. Lighting designers do not need a license or state registration.

Interior designers can also help with lighting decisions when working with you on home decor and furnishings. Some will charge a commission on purchases; others work for a fee.

When you meet with a designer, bring floor plans if you want to discuss lighting for your entire home. Where possible, bring photos of room interiors or have the designer visit your home. Many designers distinguish between design work and site visits during installation (which can be of great help). Ask for documentation with drawings, catalog pages, or technical data sheets. Get a list of all the lightbulbs and accessory parts you will need.

Clarify the services and the fee arrangement before hiring any designer. Securing competitive bids is both prudent and ethical. But remember that time is money for designers and consultants, so be fair. If you take a designer's time, be prepared to pay for it in some way.

Lighting design concerns the practical and aesthetic qualities of the light as well as the way the lighting fixtures fit into the decorating scheme.

LIGHTING DESIGN: THE FUNDAMENTAL APPROACH

Hanging a fixture in the middle of a bedroom ceiling may be customary, but it probably won't provide the best lighting for the room. The most effective approach to designing lighting schemes focuses on three basic questions: What do I want to light? How should I light it? What kind of lighting equipment and controls should I use and where should they be located? By answering these questions in that order, you will arrive at decisions that make every room in your house more comfortable.

Selecting and placing the lighting equipment is the last step because you must first determine where you need light and what effect you want to achieve. Once you have made those decisions, choosing the fixtures is relatively easy.

Lighting design isn't standardized; a good design must echo your personal preferences and the way you live in your home. If you're middle-age or older, for instance, you may need additional lighting in some places. Energy efficiency is also an important consideration.

This chapter will help you answer the three basic questions and develop a lighting design that's ideal for you.

A lighted ceiling cove and chandelier combine to create a dramatic accent in this dining room. Treat the lighting as part of the room design whenever possible, especially in new construction and remodeling.

Designing Lighting

When you plan lighting for your home, start with the fundamental questions. Draw a floor plan of the room or rooms you want to light. Indicate furniture locations and note what activities you want lighting for. Note places where activities vary, such as a dining room that's used for family meals, dinner parties with friends, and the occasional holiday buffet. Different activities usually require different lighting schemes.

WHAT DO I WANT TO LIGHT?

Day-to-day activities in your home are the major consideration in answering this question. Identify where various activities take place and what furnishings play an important role in your daily living. The more detailed your description of these activities for each area, the more effective your lighting decisions will be.

In functional, task-oriented spaces—such as a kitchen, bathroom, study, or work room—identify working surfaces, storage areas, and social zones. (Some rooms may not have social zones.) If the dining room has different service areas, such as a dining table and a buffet, each may require different lighting for those uses.

In social spaces throughout the home, such as living room and dining areas, consider the seating arrangements where people gather for conversation. Also note the cozy spots where family members go for reading, playing games, listening to music, watching television, or other pursuits. It's just as important to identify featured surfaces, furnishings, and objects you can highlight for visual interest and focus.

HOW SHOULD I LIGHT IT?

Your home's architecture and furnishings usually determine the ways you apply the

LIVING ROOM PLAN

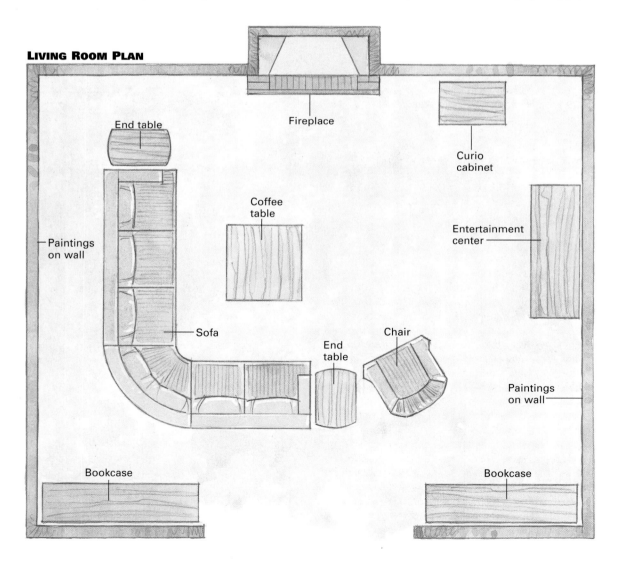

lighting effects and techniques discussed in the first chapter.

Functional areas are best served by comfortable and diffused light that is free of distracting shadows, hot spots, and glare. Countertops can be effectively lighted by fixtures underneath cabinets, which avoids body shadows. Grooming is easier when the bathroom mirror is lighted from all sides, rather than from only overhead. Local illumination should be adequate for the task, but it's important to fill the overall space with light to avoid excessive contrast with the brightest surfaces.

Lighting for social spaces depends mostly on your lifestyle, home decor, and personal preferences. Do you entertain formally or in a more relaxed fashion? Is a dramatic atmosphere in the living room your style? Or are you more comfortable in a soft and evenly lighted environment? Textured surfaces, such as a brick fireplace, look most interesting when grazed with light. Photographs and paintings look best when washed more evenly. Collectibles in display cases glow impressively when lighted with concealed display lighting. Lofty cathedral ceilings stand out when lighted indirectly; they diminish in importance when light is directed from them down into the room.

The same considerations apply to lighting outdoor spaces. Functional areas, such as patios or stairways, need even illumination. Areas of visual interest, such as a garden, benefit from a more selective use of accent lighting, with highlights and shadows. Rough surfaces, such as a stone parapet, appear most striking when grazed. Because the eye adapts to a darkened environment, overall intensity of outdoor lighting needs to be lower than that of indoor lighting.

LAYERS OF LIGHT

Lighting in any space can involve five layers of lighting:
■ Ambient lighting fills the room, providing all-around visibility for easy tasks while eliminating shadows.
■ Task lighting delivers light to specific work areas. It provides a higher level of illumination to those areas where you need it.
■ Decorative sparkle and glow provide visual focus and interest. To be effective, the lights must not be so bright that they appear harsh and uncomfortable.
■ Accent lighting highlights featured objects and surfaces, drawing attention to them and revealing interesting forms and textures. Selectively applied accent lighting prevents a room from appearing dull and uniform.
■ Wall lighting brightens vertical surfaces, drawing the eye to the perimeter of the room and enhancing the sense of spaciousness.

These five layers complement one another, and most spaces benefit from the use of multiple layers. Ambient lighting, for example, fills the shadows around the higher levels of task or accent lighting, making a work space more comfortable and a social space more attractive. Sparkle and glow set off formal areas, but their dimmed sources are best supported by a layer of ambient lighting. Wall lighting—when it reflects into the room—provides some ambient lighting. When illuminating a series of pictures, wall lighting provides highlights as well.

You can create different layers of light by using different types of fixtures. Recessed downlights, for example, can be used for ambient, task, accent, or wall lighting, depending on location and the optics of the fixture. Decorative fixtures can provide ambient lighting if they distribute light broadly or create scintillating sparkle from crystal ornaments. You have great flexibility in creating the effects you want.

A pendant fixture lights the table and ceiling, adding ambient light.

Recessed downlights provide ambient light.

Accent lighting for glassware in the cabinet also adds sparkle.

Undercabinet task lighting illuminates the countertop.

DESIGNING LIGHTING
continued

RECESSED DOWNLIGHTS PROVIDING AMBIENT LIGHT

RECESSED DOWNLIGHT WASHING A PAINTING

WHICH LIGHTING FIXTURES SHOULD I USE?

Sometimes the choice of lighting equipment is obvious—a distinctive chandelier in the dining room or a multitiered lantern in a two-story entry. Other times you have to make decisions: Is it better to highlight the fireplace with recessed accent lights or track-mounted fixtures? Will indirect light from a cove atop the kitchen cabinets be enough, or is additional lighting needed in the middle of the kitchen? The style of your furnishings is also an important consideration in your planning. The next chapter covers lighting for specific rooms, but here are some general guidelines to consider:

■ For a formal atmosphere in a traditional or contemporary home, consider prominent decorative lighting fixtures. In a modern home consider recessed lighting and orient it symmetrically to the architecture.

■ For a more relaxed atmosphere, blend different lighting effects using simple fixtures to fill the room with light.

■ For dramatic effects, use recessed or track-mounted accent lights that produce concentrated beams of light.

■ To create an atmosphere for intimate seating or comfortable reading, use a portable lamp with a diffusing shade.

You can furnish a room in a consistently traditional or modern style with decorative lighting equipment of the appropriate style. For a more eclectic decor, mix styles, playing ornate traditional pieces off the simple lines of modern ones or the soft style of contemporary designs.

■ For effective indirect lighting from a cove in a kitchen or work space, use fluorescent strip lights. In the dining room and other social areas, a low-voltage system creates softer and more easily dimmed cove lighting.

■ For comfortable grooming use well-diffused and elongated fixtures.

TABLE LAMP FOR READING

RECESSED DOWNLIGHTS WASHING WALLS

Fluorescent fixtures provide the most light while incandescent ones create a more elegant appearance that would work well in a powder room.

■ For task lighting over a countertop, install fluorescent lights for their strong and diffused light. Use tubes with good color rendition. To highlight objects on those counters and create a more social setting, use a low-voltage incandescent task light. For the larger task areas such as a laundry room, workshop, or utility area, ceiling-mounted fluorescent fixtures deliver a high level of light throughout the space.

■ To illuminate dark or intricate work, such as sewing or model making, use a portable lamp that can be placed near the task. For the desk in a home office or study, locate a comfortable reading lamp on one side of the desk. Avoid bright overhead lighting that creates distracting reflections in the screen of a computer monitor.

WHICH CONTROLS SHOULD I USE?

Install a simple on/off switch for utility or task lighting, such as in a closet or over a countertop. You can control the lights from two locations with three-way switches. To dim a single fixture or group of fixtures, install a dimmer. Preset and digital dimmers are convenient; you can turn the lights on to the intensity you want instead of adjusting them each time.

A dimming system allows you to dim an entire room of lights and create different moods or settings, as in a dining room or

living room. The push-button control allows you to reset light levels you want easily and reliably each time you use the space.

You can control lights throughout the home with a central or whole-house control, which links the switches and dimmers in each room to conveniently located keypads.

Outdoor lighting can be independently switched or integrated with your indoor lighting controls. For automatic control based on the time of day, use a timer or photocell attached to the transformer. For security lighting, a motion sensor works well.

DESIGNING LIGHTING
continued

HOW MUCH LIGHT DO YOU NEED?

The amount of light you need to see well depends on what you are looking at, how good your vision is, and how quickly and accurately you need to perform the visual task.

■ You can judge the visibility of materials by their size and contrast—how well they stand out from the background. As task visibility diminishes, lighting becomes more important. Small or intricate materials and low-contrast situations—dark thread on dark cloth, for example—require a lot of light. Bold materials or those with high contrast—such as large, black print on white paper—require less light. Good lighting becomes more important as tasks become less routine and repetitive; better vision makes it easier to see what is occurring. Good lighting and visibility are valuable when performing unfamiliar tasks.

Most household tasks fall between lighting extremes; lighting that fills a room is usually adequate for good general vision. Some activities, however, require additional light. Reading the very small print on medicine bottles (small size), judging how well-cooked

Adequate ambient light and a portable floor lamp make this basement crafts area a pleasant place to work. Light that has good color rendition is important here.

food is (low contrast), personal grooming (small size), household repairs (small size and low contrast), and hobbies are some of the areas where more light is necessary. In most cases, additional light is most effective when provided at the site.

■ The ages of people in the household is another important factor. Age often has more impact on the need for light than the requirements of the activity itself. Vision deteriorates as people get older; the effects are often most pronounced after age 50. The cornea—or lens of the eye—loses its clarity, and develops a yellow tint. The combined effect reduces the amount of light that reaches the retina. To see equally well, a 55-year-old person usually needs twice as much light as someone who is 20.

■ The speed and accuracy required when making visual decisions also affects the amount of light required. Few household tasks require instantaneous decisions. Even the most important situations around the house usually allow time for study and concentration. There are a few exceptions. Cooking often calls for a quick reaction to a visual cue: fish is done when it loses its translucency. Similar urgency applies to some hobbies—craft projects using fast-curing adhesives, for example. Providing family first aid can put pressure on a parent trying to read the label on a medicine bottle. The need for speed and accuracy in these examples compounds the difficulty of viewing things that are intrinsically hard to see, such as small or faint type.

LIGHTING LEVELS

Most people can see well under a wide range of illumination levels. Outdoor daylight varies from 5 to 10,000 foot-candles, and most people can still see under moonlight of less than one foot-candle. (The foot-candle is the standard unit for quantifying light falling on a surface.) In an intimate restaurant, table lighting is often less than 10 foot-candles. Lighting in offices and stores ranges from 30 to 200 foot-candles, but demanding visual tasks such as drafting or dentistry require 200 to 1,000 foot-candles.

Home lighting needs are fairly modest, from 5 foot-candles in hallways to 200 foot-candles in task areas—a home office, sewing room, or workshop, for example.

While lighting levels in different types of commercial, industrial, and institutional spaces are usually specified in terms of foot-candles, such recommendations are largely impractical—and unnecessary—in the home. Filling the room with light to eliminate shadows and providing supplemental light for difficult tasks and imperfect vision is usually sufficient. Specific recommendations in this book refer to the wattage of light sources as a guide to achieving effective illumination.

Outdoor vision differs because your eyes quickly adapt to the lower level of brightness in the nighttime environment. Much less light is needed to create contrast with darkened surroundings—most people find it easy to read under a full moon, once they are accustomed to the darkness. The most common lighting problem outdoors is having too much light in some areas and not enough in others. This imbalance prevents the eye from adapting comfortably and causes people to search out local pools of light.

LIGHTING FOR HEALTH AND WELL-BEING

A cheery, well-lighted room may not actually improve your health, but it will make you feel better when days grow short.

How light affects health is a subject of increasing popular and scientific interest. Studies have been made of the amount of light needed to see well in various circumstances and methods for controlling light to avoid discomfort. There is less solid data available about broader issues of health and well-being.

Reflectorized bulb in recessed housing reduces glare for more comfortable lighting.

SEASONAL AFFECTIVE DISORDER

Sometimes known as winter depression, seasonal affective disorder (SAD) is related to the production and suppression of melatonin in the hypothalamus gland, which is sensitive to day-night cycles and the amount of daylight the eyes receive. Jet lag of travelers and weariness of shift-changing workers are other problems related to disruptions of the biological clock and circadian rhythms.

Studies have found that melatonin regulation is sensitive to the amount of light received, but not to the spectral composition (color) of the light. Most professionals are skeptical of health benefits claimed for full-spectrum light sources. It's not practical to use built-in residential lighting to provide the high levels of illumination and concentrated viewing time needed to counteract SAD. Portable lighting to combat SAD is available, but—as with any health therapy—you should consult a medical professional before use.

ULTRAVIOLET RADIATION

Ultraviolet radiation, particularly shortwave UV-B radiation, can damage the skin, especially of children. The most significant source of UV radiation is sunlight. Many guidelines and protective skin products help people limit outdoor UV exposure. Fluorescent and halogen lights also emit UV radiation, but at much lower levels than sunlight. Glass used in most fluorescent bulbs and tubes absorbs UV, further reducing UV-exposure danger from electric light. Constant exposure to common levels of fluorescent lighting—equivalent to a few hours of sunlight—is not as threatening.

Halogen light sources, however, are usually enclosed in quartz glass, which does not absorb UV radiation. Instead a separate hard glass filter is required, either as part of the light source or as part of the fixture.

HEAT

Light sources generate heat, and many are hot to the touch. The heat is proportional to the wattage of the source, but even low-wattage bulbs can be painfully hot to unprotected skin. The smaller the source, the more concentrated the heat, and the hotter it feels. Small, high-wattage sources can be hazardous. Guidelines that govern the manufacture of lighting equipment are mostly concerned with fire prevention and electrical safety, so it is up to the user to avoid contact with lighting

Tiny incandescent bulbs like these may be too hot for youngsters to touch. Shielded bulbs or fluorescent undercabinet lights might be better for homes with young children.

fixtures that may be too hot to touch. It is important to protect toddlers and children from all bulbs, but especially from low-voltage undercabinet task lights, high-intensity table lamps, and other small, high-wattage bulbs.

DISCOMFORT AROUND FLUORESCENT LIGHTING

The flicker of fluorescent lighting annoys some people. Sensitivity varies considerably from person to person. Sometimes flicker complaints are part of a wider dislike for the color, glare, and flat light put out by poor fluorescent lighting installations. Magnetic ballasts commonly found in older and cheaper fluorescent fixtures often cause flickering. Today's electronic ballasts operate at high frequency and virtually eliminate flicker; most people find them comfortable.

LIGHTING FOR OLDER EYES

In addition to needing more light to see well, people in their 50s and beyond are also more sensitive to glare. Tiny fissures in the cornea caused by aging break up light into tiny pinpricks of glare, making bright light sources especially uncomfortable. This makes providing adequate light even more challenging. To minimize glare thoroughly conceal light sources in the ceiling or behind fascias and carefully shield exposed light sources with diffusing shades. Locating lights close to tasks also reduces glare around the room.

The yellowing of the cornea filters out blue light, which tends to make vision muddy or lacking in contrast, especially where lighting is from warm, incandescent sources. Fluorescent light—which is richer in blue light—can help offset this problem.

Textures and colors are important in cooking. As eyes age, more light is needed in the kitchen as in other rooms.

ENERGY-EFFICIENT LIGHTING

Residential lighting consumes a lot of electricity, sometimes as much as one-third of the electricity used in a home. (Depending on the energy sources in the home, the rest may be used for cooling and heating, heating water, cooking, washing dishes and clothes, and running small appliances.) Electricity use not only costs you on your utility bill, it also contributes to environmental pollution through the burning of fossil fuels. So saving electricity benefits you while helping the environment.

Energy-efficient lighting meets your lighting needs while consuming the least amount of energy. Lighting that conserves energy but does not provide the quantity or quality of light you want is ineffective and even wasteful.

Energy is power consumed over time. So you can conserve energy by reducing the

Portable lighting such as the table lamp on the desk and the reading lights beside the bed are ideal for directing light where you need it.

Light-colored finishes and a reflective shade on the fixture over the table make this dining nook bright without using a lot of electricity.

Reflectorized bulbs like the ones at right concentrate light on specific areas.

amount of lighting power (watts) you use or the length of time you use it. To reduce the time you use lighting, turn off (or dim) the light when you do not need it.

For energy-efficient lighting put light only where you need it, use light-colored finishes in rooms, use efficient light sources and fixtures and use lighting controls.

PUT LIGHT WHERE YOU NEED IT

The layered lighting approach discussed on page 37 saves energy. By using local task lighting, you avoid a uniform and wasteful level of intense light throughout the home. Only those areas that need a lot of light receive it; the rest are illuminated at a lower (more comfortable and attractive) level. To save energy with accent lighting, place the light source close to the target and use a bulb with lower wattage.

USE LIGHT-COLOR FINISHES

Dark ceilings, walls, and countertops can absorb up to four times as much light as lighter surfaces. Because a lot of light reaches a surface directly, without reflection, a space with dark finishes may require twice as much light—still a major loss in efficiency. Of course dark finishes add visual interest to your home, but using them selectively, especially in task areas, will help you use less lighting to see comfortably.

ENERGY-EFFICIENT LIGHTING
continued

USE EFFICIENT LIGHT SOURCES

Fluorescent light sources generate up to five times as much light per watt as most incandescent ones. Where you need a lot of light in one area, such as on a kitchen counter, around a bathroom mirror, or in an office, fluorescent lights are a good choice.

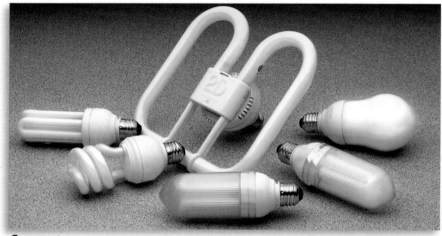

Compact fluorescent lamps (above) screw into standard fixtures to replace incandescent bulbs. They can provide the same light level while using less electricity.

Low-wattage lamps are adequate for task lighting under cabinets because they are close to the work surface and the light is directed to the task.

Because fluorescent sources last longer than incandescent, maintenance costs will be less, too. Fluorescent lights also serve well where lights operate for long periods of time, such as in a rear entry. (Compact fluorescent bulbs work particularly well here.) While halogen sources are more efficient than ordinary incandescent ones, the difference is not as significant. You can compare the efficiency of incandescent light sources by comparing the lumens per watt number on lightbulb packages—a larger number indicates a more efficient bulb.

USE EFFICIENT LIGHTING FIXTURES

Light sources in the home should be shielded to prevent glare. (A bare light source, while 100 percent efficient, glares and is unsightly.) Most shielding, however, absorbs— and therefore wastes—light. This can be a major problem with recessed fixtures, which trap light inside the fixture. Better fixtures have polished reflectors that direct light down into the space; they can use lower-wattage bulbs because more of the light reaches the room. Look for wall and ceiling fixtures with a smaller opaque housing and a bigger luminous diffuser or an open top; they emit more light.

USE LIGHTING CONTROLS

Turning off lights when you do not need them or reducing power to them when appropriate will save energy. Lighting controls include the simple on/off switch and automatic controls, such as timers and motion sensors. Central control systems allow you to turn lights on and off throughout the house from one location and indicate where lights have been left on throughout the home.

Dimmers let you reduce light levels and reduce energy consumption where activities or particular users need less illumination. Dimmers save energy and prolong the life of incandescent lightbulbs, which saves on maintenance as well.

COMPARATIVE LIGHTING COSTS, 10-YEAR TOTAL EXPENSE

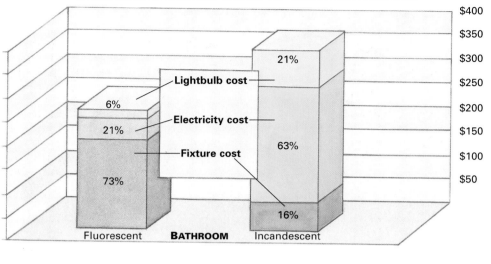

$400
$350
$300
$250
$200
$150
$100
$50

21%

6%

Lightbulb cost

21%

Electricity cost

63%

Fixture cost

73%

16%

Fluorescent **BATHROOM** Incandescent

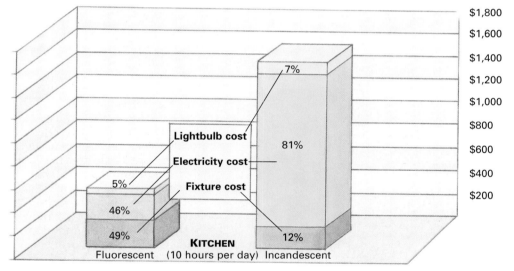

$1,800
$1,600
$1,400
$1,200
$1,000
$800
$600
$400
$200

7%

Lightbulb cost

81%

Electricity cost

5%

Fixture cost

46%

49%

12%

Fluorescent **KITCHEN** (10 hours per day) Incandescent

RETROFIT COMPACT FLUORESCENT LAMPS

INDOOR LIGHTING IDEAS

Indirect cove lighting and direct lighting from the fan combine with floor lamps to make this media room comfortable and inviting. Recessed fixtures in the ceiling perimeter, not shown in this view, illuminate built-in cabinetry and add ambient light.

This chapter shows how to light each room of your home. For a new home, use the architectural drawings to lay out your ideas and develop the lighting plan. Most copy centers now offer large-format reproductions so you can make clean copies of the floor plan or enlarge plans of specific rooms.

If you want to add or improve lighting in an existing home, simply measure the dimensions and sketch the layout in an appropriate scale, placing doors and windows on your plan. Locate your furniture on the plan (to scale, as much as possible) or purchase an inexpensive furniture template at an art supply store. Consider the uses and activities of each room, as well as the lighting effects and styles you are interested in achieving.

Sparkling candle bulbs make this two-tier chandelier twinkle. Coordinating wall sconces are mounted high so the unshielded bulbs won't glare in the eyes of people at the table.

THE ENTRY FOYER

The entry foyer—a home's first impression—serves as a staging area when entering and leaving the home. Here you may greet visitors, find or place clothing in a closet, check your appearance in a mirror, or scan mail. Incandescent bulbs, with their warm and inviting tones, provide the most welcoming effect.

It's hard to imagine a palatial entry foyer like this without a large chandelier. A hanging fixture adds elegance to any tall space.

AT THE FRONT DOOR

A single decorative fixture usually provides enough illumination in a small area if the light is well-diffused. Concentrated overhead lighting creates disturbing shadows on the faces of guests. Choose a fixture that is the right size for the space; one that's 15–20 inches in diameter, with two or three 60-watt bulbs, usually works well. Where ceiling height permits (or dictates), hang a pendant fixture. A pendant centered in a transom window over the front door pleasantly highlights the doorway.

If the main light is in front of a closet, you will be able to see inside it. Otherwise provide a light inside the closet or a recessed downlight in front of it. (See page 66 for tips on closet lights and pages 26–27 for downlighting suggestions.)

If you have a side mirror or table, dress up the foyer lighting with a pair of flanking wall sconces or table lamps. They won't, however, fill the space with light by themselves. Sconces look balanced on most walls when they are mounted at eye level—about 5 feet, 6 inches above the floor. Keep the wattage relatively low; a 60- or 75-watt bulb will be fine. If you are using a tall sconce, check the electrical box location (it may not be centered) so you can position it correctly in the wall.

TALL SPACES

A longer pendant, such as a multitiered lantern or chandelier, is a good choice for installation in a double-height entry. A dimmer will soften the light from the bare bulb and extend its life. Be sure your fixture dealer provides enough chain or cord to hang the fixture at the desired height—ideally, either centered in a window or midway in the space. Fixtures installed on or in the ceiling will be difficult to maintain in a tall space and may not provide sufficient light.

LARGE FOYERS

In larger foyers a single fixture may look inadequate and leave shadows in transition areas. Augment the fixture with wall sconces, smaller ceiling fixtures, or recessed downlights as the entry transitions into the interior of the home. Decorative fixtures that match the style of the central fixture add to the formality of the space and keep the design from becoming too busy. Control the supplemental fixtures and the central fixture with separate dimmers so you can balance their brightness. Separate controls also allow you to leave only one layer illuminated when the space is not occupied. For more convenience, install three-way dimmers or switches in a large foyer so you can control lights at the front door as well as at the foyer entryway to the home.

INTERIOR HALLS AND STAIRWAYS

Long halls are most comfortable when lighted evenly throughout. The hallway needs enough lighting fixtures to spread the light, but not a lot of light overall. Locate fixtures where hallways intersect and set them 6 to 8 feet apart. Small, well diffused decorative fixtures or recessed downlights with 60- or 75-watt A bulbs give a wide beam. (To highlight art in the hall, see page 61.) Where lights are on throughout the day, fixtures with compact fluorescent lamps will be more economical to operate and will last 10 times as long as incandescent bulbs.

Stairways need lights on the landings and the steps for safety. Fixtures at the top and bottom will usually provide enough light and will contribute to the hallway lighting as well.

Hallways are ideal places for three-way controls that you can operate from either end. Install dimmers for incandescent fixtures to extend lamp life and to provide an overnight setting.

Recessed downlights wash walls and light the floor in a hallway.

A ceiling fixture that matches the style of the house is a good choice for entry lighting.

A chandelier is in scale with a tall entry.

THE KITCHEN

Lighting under the cabinets casts even illumination across the countertops in this kitchen. You never stand in the way of your work light with this kind of lighting.

Often the center of activity in an American home, the kitchen is a place for both functional and social activities. Key visual tasks include food preparation, cooking, and cleanup; and storage and retrieval of groceries, cooking utensils, and dinnerware. Sometimes the kitchen is a place for reading, doing homework, and taking care of household business. Social activities range from conversation over a cup of coffee to family meals in a dining area. Guests often gather in the kitchen too.

The layered lighting approach lets you provide task lighting for each work area while ambient lighting fills the kitchen and accent lighting highlights special features.

TASK LIGHTING FOR COUNTERTOPS

Countertops are best lighted with fluorescent or low-voltage incandescent task lights mounted under the cabinets. Undercabinet lights cover the work surface without casting body shadows or overhead glare. Fluorescent fixtures deliver more light, but be sure to use tubes with good color rendition. Incandescent fixtures cast warmer light that some prefer.

Undercabinet task lights are available with a cord and plug for retrofit installation or with a splice box for direct wiring in new construction or renovation. A switch on the fixture provides local control, or several fixtures can be connected and controlled from a single wall switch. Low-voltage systems include a jumper harness to connect fixtures. They can be dimmed with a compatible (electronic low-voltage) dimmer.

Mount the task lights under the cabinets near the front edge so the light adequately covers the primary work area. You can install a continuous line of lights over the counter or put in one fixture per cabinet, depending on the cabinet design. The sides of American-style cabinets extend below the bottom, so you must install separate fixtures on each one, sized to fit within the width of each cabinet. European-style cabinets have sides flush with the bottom, so fixtures can be placed anywhere beneath them. Have a plan of your cabinetry available when selecting the undercabinet lighting. If you are using a cord- and-plug model, attach the cords to the bottom of the cabinets with staples or adhesive wire clips.

Shield undercabinet task lights behind a fascia—a narrow board along the bottom front of the cabinet. In most cases the cabinet

SELECTING THE STYLE OF DOWNLIGHT

White baffles are popular because they blend into the usually white-painted ceiling. When illuminated, however, a white baffle reflects rather than absorbs stray light, which can cause glare. In a large, open kitchen where you see much of the ceiling, light from a black baffle will be more pleasing.

Natural aluminum reflectors are efficient and provide comfortable light. They blend well with chrome and stainless steel appliances, but may appear too modern for traditional interiors.

Fully enclosed downlights are another option. The lens is easy to clean, but the lights may appear too institutional to fit into some kitchen styles.

face frames or doors act as the fascias. If not you can add one yourself. A fascia 2 inches deep will hide the lights unless you are sitting close to the counter. If you do sit at the counter, locate the task lights at the back of the cabinets. The counter lighting will not be as effective, but light at the seating area will be more comfortable.

OTHER TASK LOCATIONS

SINK: An undercabinet task light over the sink helps you see into deep pots. Where the cabinets extend over the sink and water from the sink may splash upwards, a fluorescent strip light works best. If there is no cabinet, place a single downlight over the sink, either a recessed light or a surface-mounted cylinder with a 75-watt reflector bulb.

Another choice is to mount a fluorescent strip light behind a 6-inch-deep valance that spans the sink. Locate the light flush with the top of the valance to hide it from view.

Hard-wired lights over the sink can be controlled together with the ambient lighting or switched separately.

ISLAND OR PENINSULA: Recessed downlights in the ceiling are effective over peninsulas and island counters where there are no overhanging cabinets. Locate the lights 2 to 3 feet apart, centered over the work surface. Where a peninsula serves as a dining area, small decorative pendants with metal shades or glass diffusers can add character to the kitchen. Suspend the fixtures so they do not block your vision when standing or seated at the counter—about 6 feet above the floor is usually a good height. Many pendant fixtures can be mounted on tracks, which simplifies installation, especially in a retrofit. You will need the appropriate adapters for your fixtures and track. Install a dimmer control.

STOVE OR RANGE: Ovens and most range hoods have built-in lighting. It may not be enough for some people, however, so be sure that ambient lighting effectively illuminates the area above and in front of the stove.

A freestanding island with a downward-vented cooktop presents the same challenges as a peninsula. Locate two or four recessed downlights above the sides of the island, where smoke and spatter from the cooking will not float directly up into them.

DINING NOOK: A decorative pendant provides comfortable and pleasant light over a small table. Choose one with a frosted bulb (100 or 150 watts) and a metal shade or a glass or plastic diffuser. Bare or clear bulbs will be too harsh. Pendant lighting is comfortable for homework and general reading. Suspend the fixture so it does not block your view across the table—about 30 inches above the tabletop is usually enough. Add wall sconces to enhance the lighting, but don't rely on them alone to light the area. Lighting in the nook should be controlled with a separate dimmer.

PANTRY: You need enough light in a pantry to read the small print on product labels. Otherwise you have to carry items to the kitchen to read the labels. In an enclosed pantry a two-tube fluorescent fixture on the ceiling provides ample, well-diffused light. Center the fixture in the space and provide a switch beside the door.

If the pantry is open to the rest of the kitchen, you can light the area with the same kind of fixtures you use for ambient lighting to maintain continuity. Place them about 6 feet apart. You don't need a separate control unless the pantry is a distinct space.

UNDERCABINET TASK LIGHTING

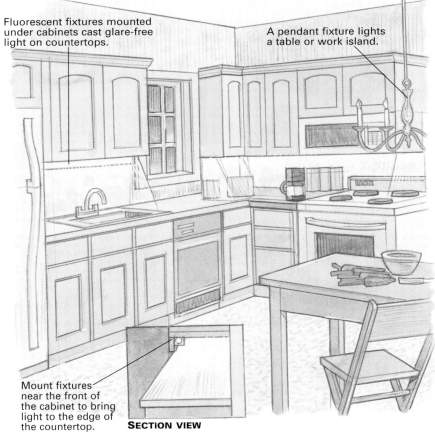

Fluorescent fixtures mounted under cabinets cast glare-free light on countertops.

A pendant fixture lights a table or work island.

Mount fixtures near the front of the cabinet to bring light to the edge of the countertop.

SECTION VIEW

THE KITCHEN
continued

AMBIENT LIGHTING

Ambient lighting illuminates cabinets, provides for overall visibility, and fills in around your task lighting to minimize shadows. Many choices are available, depending on the look you want.

Allow 2½ to 3 watts (incandescent) per square foot. (In a 10×15-foot kitchen, this is 400 to 450 watts—five or six 75-watt bulbs.) Because the heat of incandescent bulbs limits the wattage you can install in a fixture, you may need several fixtures.

RECESSED DOWNLIGHTS: Recessed downlighting is unobtrusive. It blends with many styles of architecture and cabinet design and leaves the visual focus on those elements and other decorative lighting. Downlights are also a good choice when the kitchen is open to the dining or family room and will be seen from those spaces.

A 5-inch-diameter downlight is a good choice for ceilings 9 feet tall or less. To avoid glare, the light should have a reflector or baffle that places the lightbulb well above the ceiling. Use a 75-watt A or BR flood bulb; spot and PAR lamps create a shadowy, concentrated beam that is hard to work under. Some 5-inch downlights and most 7-inch ones are rated for 100-watt bulbs. Install these in rooms that are larger or have higher ceilings; they will overpower a small room.

Compact fluorescent lamps (CFL) are common in recessed downlights for commercial spaces. For residential use, choose a downlight designed for a CFL. It will include a plug-in (not screw-in) socket and a ballast. Some screw-in retrofit CFLs fit into downlights, but they usually protrude, which looks unattractive and creates glare.

Locate downlights 12 to 18 inches from the faces of cabinets, measured to the center of the fixture. At 12 inches, more light falls on the countertops, but the lights can create hot spots or scallops on cabinet doors. The 18-inch spacing works better in taller ceilings.

Space the downlights 4 to 6 feet apart in a regular pattern. Spacing

Pendant fixtures light the cooking and preparation island in this kitchen. Recessed downlights around the edges provide additional ambient light.

near the low end of the range works best in a small kitchen, one with dark finishes, or where you want higher light levels. Use the wider spacing in larger kitchens or those with light finishes.

Control the downlights with a dimmer, and install three- or four-way switches at each entry to the kitchen.

DECORATIVE CEILING AND PENDANT FIXTURES: When part of the kitchen is primarily a social space, consider installing decorative incandescent fixtures that complement the decor. If the ceiling is at least 9 feet tall, hang a pendant or a fixture close to the ceiling. The fixture should have uplight distribution to spread the light around the room. Otherwise look for shallow, well-diffused fixtures. Control the fixtures with a dimmer, using three- or four-way devices at each entry to the kitchen.

AMBIENT LIGHTING

Recessed lights in ceiling

A pendant fixture or chandelier fixture over the table adds ambient light.

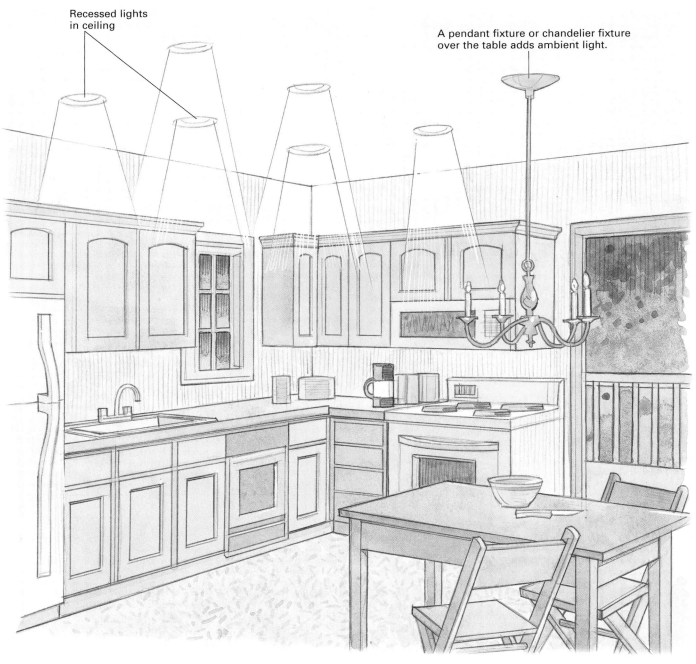

THE KITCHEN
continued

Lighting above, below, and inside these cabinets creates a preparation space that doubles as a sparkling serving area for entertaining.

CEILING MOUNTED FLUORESCENT FIXTURE: A large fluorescent fixture provides a lot of light from a single location. It is usually the most economical way to light a kitchen. This approach is particularly effective for a functional kitchen that is not open to dining or social areas.

Fluorescent lighting works well in a kitchen with a low ceiling because the fixtures are shallower than incandescent lights. Typical fluorescent fixtures extend 5 inches or less from the ceiling.

Fixtures with wraparound or cloud diffusers distribute some light onto the ceiling, which brightens the space and reduces glare. Fixtures with opaque sides direct all light downward, so they do not reveal defects in the ceiling. Wood or metal louvers on the face of some fixtures are more than decorative; they hide hot spots on the diffuser.

A nominal 2×4-foot fixture holds four tubes and can illuminate an area of about 150 square feet. In a smaller room use a 2×2 or 1×4 fixture with two tubes. Install several fixtures in a large kitchen. All fixtures should have tubes with good color rendition. Connect fluorescent ceiling lighting to a separate switch. Install three- or four-way switches for convenience when the kitchen has two or three entries.

COVE LIGHTING: Indirect lighting from cabinet tops creates a pleasant environment that's closer to a naturally lighted space than downlighting. The light often seems muted, however, so it is usually supplemented with accent lighting or decorative fixtures.

For the best light spread, the kitchen ceiling, walls, and cabinets should have light-color finishes. There should be at least 18 inches above the cabinets. A kitchen less than 12 feet wide can be lighted from one side; larger spaces should be lighted from opposite coves.

Install a single-lamp, 4-foot fluorescent strip light for every 25 to 30 square feet of kitchen area. (That's 13 to 16 lights in a 20×20-foot kitchen.) Place the fixtures in continuous rows, leaving any extra space at the ends, rather than between the fixtures. All the strip lights should be the same length and should have tubes that provide good color rendition.

Install a fascia 3½ inches high on top of the cabinet frame. Place the edge of the fluorescent strip light 1 inch from the fascia and, if necessary, shim it until the top of the tube is level with the top of the fascia. Butt the strip lights together end-to-end and wire them together. Provide a separate switch for all the cove lighting, using three- or four-way switches if the kitchen has multiple entries.

Low-voltage cove lighting supplements ambient lighting well. (See page 27.)

Fluorescent cove lighting above cabinets lights the ceiling for accent and to increase ambient light.

DIMMING FLUORESCENT FIXTURES

Dimming incandescent light sources is simple, inexpensive, and produces a pleasing warm glow. There are times, though, when you need the high light output of fluorescent lamps along with the flexibility of a dimmer control. Unlike incandescent lamps, fluorescent lamps do not last longer when they are dimmed. The light's color may shift to a slightly bluish tint as it dims.

Dimming a fluorescent fixture requires a special dimming ballast and a compatible fluorescent dimmer control. The ballast and dimmer may be manufactured by the same company, or they may be the products of different manufacturers that are listed to work together. Some dimming ballasts work on standard two-conductor wiring and are suitable for retrofit installation. Others require additional control wires, which complicates installation. Check the manufacturer's specifications. Look for a dimming ballast that has been factory-tuned to prevent flickering at low intensity.

Don't install an incandescent dimmer control with fluorescent lighting, and don't put incandescent and fluorescent fixtures on the same circuit with a fluorescent dimmer.

KITCHEN LIGHTING PLAN

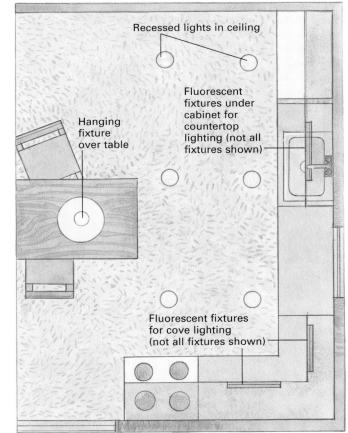

Recessed lights in ceiling

Fluorescent fixtures under cabinet for countertop lighting (not all fixtures shown)

Hanging fixture over table

Fluorescent fixtures for cove lighting (not all fixtures shown)

THE DINING ROOM

A chandelier over the table and portable lamps on the sideboard give intimate lighting for dinner with friends. Candles on the table will light diners' faces

A dining room might host either formal or informal gatherings. And it often becomes a place for doing homework, household bookkeeping and correspondence, or hobbies. The dining room table is the focal point of the room, so lighting layers are built around it. The more activities you have in your dining room, the more layers of light the room will probably need.

THE CENTRAL CHANDELIER

The first layer of light is usually a chandelier or pendant centered over the table. Select a fixture that matches the size of the room and the table. A fixture 24 to 30 inches in diameter generally fits an average dining room comfortably. If the room is narrower than 10 feet, look for a smaller fixture. The diameter of a chandelier should be at least 12 inches less than the width of the table, or it will crowd the diners.

Suspend the chandelier high enough so that diners can see each other under it. With an 8-foot ceiling, the fixture should hang 30 inches above the table. To preserve the proportions in a room with higher ceilings, raise the chandelier 3 inches for each additional foot of ceiling height.

Chandeliers usually come with at least 3 feet of chain and cord. But you should verify that the model you want will hang correctly in your space. Shortening the chain is simple. You can pry open the links, remove the excess length, and cut the power cord.

Control the chandelier with a dimmer. Dim crystal chandeliers and those with exposed bulbs to a pleasing glow. Uplight pendants can be operated at higher intensity because most of their light reflects off the ceiling.

Sconces flank breakfront

30"

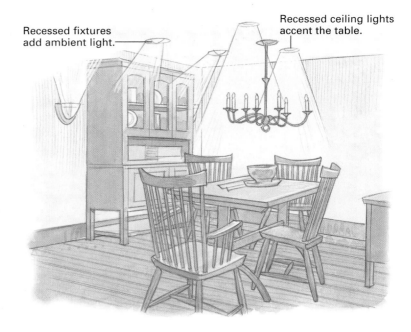

Recessed fixtures add ambient light.

Recessed ceiling lights accent the table.

ACCENT LIGHT FOR THE TABLE

The dimmed chandelier will light diners' faces comfortably, but will not cast much light on the tabletop. To bring out the sparkle in table settings and centerpieces, add accent lighting. The accent lights can be recessed or track-mounted, located midway between the center of the table and the ends. If you have a larger chandelier that might create shadows, push the accent lights farther away from the middle of the table. To avoid unflattering shadows, place the accent lights or downlights so they aren't over the diners' heads. Fixtures 3 to 4 inches in diameter are unobtrusive. Those with low-voltage 20- to 50-watt MR16 lamps or a 50-watt PAR20 are good choices. Lamps with medium or flood distribution prevent hot spots on the table.

WALL LIGHTING

Make your dining space more comfortable and attractive by lighting the walls. For this third layer in your lighting composition, choose a featured area—such as a buffet or sideboard, breakfront, or a wall with a painting or drapery—to focus your lighting on. Narrow candlestick table lamps on top of the buffet, wall sconces over it, or accent light from above all provide pleasing light for a buffet. For a formal atmosphere select lights that match the style of the chandelier. The accent lights can be the same type as you use over the table. (For tips on lighting a glass breakfront, paintings, and drapes, see pages 61–63.)

AMBIENT LIGHTING

In a large dining room, add light around the table and fill the space with a soft brightness. In a small room the wall lighting will provide adequate ambient light. Recessed downlights between the table and the corners of the room provide comfortable ambient lighting without dominating the room. You can use small accent fixtures, aimed down, or 5-inch downlights similar to the ones discussed in the kitchen section. (See page 52.)

DIMMING CONTROLS

To adjust the intensity of each layer of lighting to a pleasing balance, dim each one separately. Make sure you control the central chandelier with a separate dimmer. Other lights can be combined or placed on separate dimmers. A dimming system (described on page 65) works well in a dining room. If there are two entries to a large dining room, put a three-way control at each entry.

DINING ROOM LIGHTING PLAN

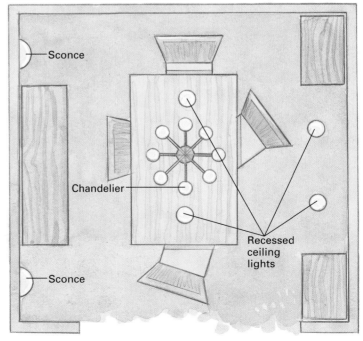

Sconce

Chandelier

Sconce

Recessed ceiling lights

THE LIVING ROOM

The living room is the principal place for conversation and social activities in most homes. Reading, playing games, listening to music, and watching television are typical of the visual tasks that go on here. Establishing a comfortable atmosphere is usually the top priority in selecting living-room lighting.

VISUAL ORGANIZATION

Spaces look most attractive when the lighting appears visually organized and integrated with the rest of the furnishings. First find the visual focus of the room—it might be a fireplace, books on shelves, a painting, a seating area, or a media center. In a large room you may have more than one area, each with its own focal point. Build the lighting plan around the visual focus, using layers of ambient, accent, and wall lighting.

RECESSED OR TRACK ACCENT LIGHTING: For accent and wall lighting, use either recessed or track-mounted accent lights. Recessed fixtures are less conspicuous, but they are more difficult and costly to install. Once recessed fixtures are in place, they are difficult to move and most cannot be aimed. Track lighting stands out and is visible on the ceiling, but it is flexible and easy to install. You can adjust track lighting and move the fixtures if you rearrange the room.

LIGHTING A FIREPLACE: If the fireplace has a chimney of rough stone or brick, light it to bring out the texture. Locate two accent lights (recessed or track-mounted) about 12 inches away from the surface and centered on it. Aim the lights so the beams rake down the chimney, creating highlights and shadows on the rough surface. Light will also fall on the hearth and mantel, illuminating fireplace implements and other decorative elements. Use small fixtures with 50-watt MR16 or PAR20 bulbs in a baffled, reflector, or pinhole downlight (an eyeball style extends below the ceiling) or compact, low-profile track fixtures.

Halogen spotlights mounted on rods wash the painting over the fireplace and the ceiling (top). Recessed ceiling fixtures provide ambient light in the living room at left.

If the fireplace is in the wall, highlight art on the wall or objects on the mantel. Locate the accent lights 18 to 30 inches from the wall to keep the light from grazing the surface. (Grazing light reveals nailheads and other imperfections in a wall.) Use wide-beam bulbs to illuminate art and narrow beams to highlight small objects.

LIGHTING PAINTINGS: To highlight a long wall with several paintings, light it with a relatively even wash. Locate the lights 18 to 30 inches from the wall an equal distance apart. Close spacing softens the shadows at the top of the wall (called scallops). Recessed wall-washer fixtures distribute light up to the top of the wall and cast a smooth beam on the wall. Use 75- or 100-watt bulbs. Wall washers trap a lot of light, so lower-wattage bulbs may work in some situations.

Another approach is to run track lighting parallel to the wall. Light the wall with small track fixtures and wide-beam bulbs. Space the fixtures about 24 inches apart. Smoothing lenses are available for many track fixtures to make the lighting more even. Recessed wall washers give the smoothest effect. For a more dramatic effect, cluster the lights and aim them at individual paintings.

Recessed accent lights highlight this fireplace wall and painting.

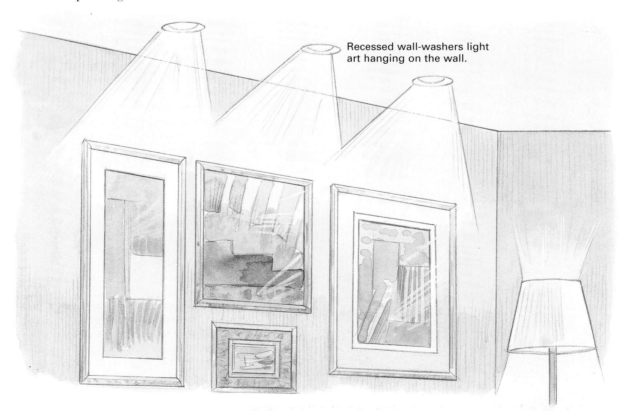

Recessed wall-washers light art hanging on the wall.

THE LIVING ROOM
continued

Wall-washers provide soft lighting for watching the large-screen television. Christmas tree lights above dark blue acrylic ceiling panels add sparkle.

Ceiling fan with light

Portable floor lamp for reading

LIGHTING DRAPERIES: Grazing light at a steep angle highlights the texture and color of draperies and other window coverings. Position accent lights 12 inches away from the surface and 12 inches apart. Use 50-watt MR16 or PAR20 narrow-beam bulbs (as recommended for the fireplace). A one-tube fluorescent strip light behind a valance lights window treatments well. Use the same length strip for all valances. You can locate track lights behind a valance, but keep the fixtures at least 6 inches from any fabric or combustible material.

LIGHTING A SEATING AREA: Table and floor lamps with linen shades make a comfortable and attractive pool of light at the ends of a sofa or seating area. Choose a lamp that will light people's faces without glaring into the eyes of people seated nearby.

A lamp with a metal reflector makes a good reading light. It does not create a warm and friendly glow, however, so put it beside a separate reading chair. When a portable lamp will be in the middle of a large room, install a floor receptacle so

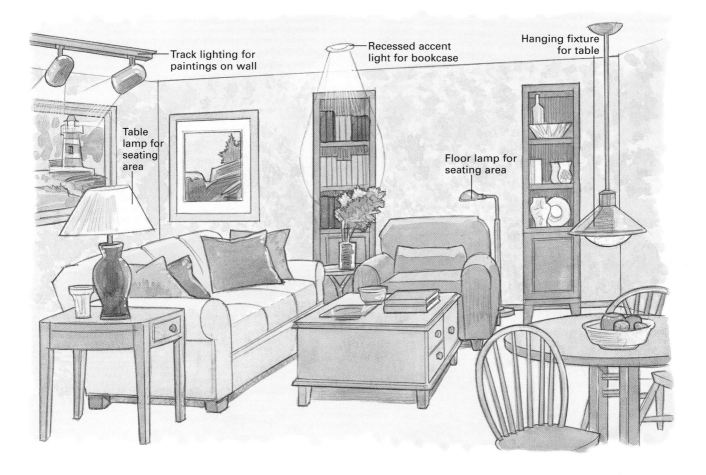

Track lighting for paintings on wall

Recessed accent light for bookcase

Hanging fixture for table

Table lamp for seating area

Floor lamp for seating area

people won't trip over the lamp cord.

To light a wall with seating against it, locate recessed or track lights 18 to 24 inches from the wall. They should not beam down on people seated under them.

Center a single downlight over a coffee table. Arrange nearby downlights so they form a geometric pattern in the ceiling.

LIGHTING A DISPLAY CABINET:
Aim an accent light into a display cabinet to illuminate the objects inside. For a cabinet that's 72 inches tall or less, measure from the ceiling down to the center of the display area. That's the vertical aiming distance. Locate the accent light on the ceiling, half of that distance from the face of the cabinet. To light up the entire display area, use a wide-beam lamp in the accent light. Install two accent lights for cabinets wider than 48 inches.

Or you can install miniature accent lighting in the cabinet. Cabinet accent lights are shallow disks about 3 inches in diameter with 10- or 20-watt, low-voltage bulbs. They mount in a hole in a shelf or attach directly to the surface. A plug-in transformer can supply up to 60 watts. Three lights, a transformer, and lead wires are usually available as a kit.

The cabinet must have enough space to conceal the low-voltage transformer. You must also be able to hide the low-voltage wiring. Control the lights by plugging them into a receptacle wired to a wall switch; or you can install a switch in the transformer cord. The lights are not compatible with room-light dimmers.

LIGHTING A MEDIA CENTER: A television screen does not need to be lighted to be visible. In fact it is easier to see the screen when no light falls directly on it. However many people prefer television viewing in a well-lighted environment where they can see family members or guests, read, or perform other tasks—multitasking has become a part of home life.

For balanced lighting around the media center, place lights on either side of the TV screen. This keeps glare off the screen and gives enough light to read the titles of material in the media cabinet. Locate recessed or track lights 18 to 24 inches from the cabinet face to illuminate the bottom shelves. Space the lights 18 to 24 inches apart for adequate coverage. Wash paintings above the cabinet from the same location.

THE LIVING ROOM
continued

Cove lighting highlights the vaulted wood ceiling in the room shown above. The same type of lighting is an effective indirect ambient light source in the room at top right; floor and table lamps provide reading light and establish social areas. Craftsman style bracket fixtures built into banded ceiling trim (right) contribute both light and style to the room.

CEILING FANS

An attractive fan often becomes the visual focus in a room that lacks other features. A ceiling fan cools in the summer and reverses to help warm in the winter. The fan moves air around the room but does not change the air temperature. When the blades turn counterclockwise, air moves directly downward. The breeze on your skin can make you feel up to 6 degrees cooler, so you can set the thermostat higher, saving as much as 30 to 40 percent of air-conditioning costs. When the blades turn clockwise, they mix the air, distributing warmer air that rises and collects near the ceiling down where people sit and stand.

A 56-inch fan is effective in rooms up to 400 square feet. A larger room requires a larger fan or multiple fans. (See page 94 for installation instructions.) A wireless remote control, available built-in or as an accessory, eliminates the need to have pull-strings for switches hanging into the room.

AMBIENT LIGHTING

A living room is most pleasant when it is filled with light. If your living room has portable lamps around seating areas, wall lighting, and accent lights, additional ambient light may be unnecessary. In larger rooms some fill-in light will help avoid shadows and dark corners.

A ceiling fan with a light kit will gently illuminate the center of the room. The fan-light combination will not, however, light up the edges of the room.

Recessed downlights can also add ambient light. Arrange them in a geometric pattern in the middle of the space, 4 to 6 feet apart. Small, low-voltage fixtures with 50-watt bulbs create crisp, dramatic lighting. Standard downlights with 60- or 75-watt bulbs provide a softer, more comfortable atmosphere. Use wide-beam bulbs in both cases and choose fixtures that are well-shielded with deep baffles or reflectors to avoid glare.

LIGHTING A CATHEDRAL CEILING:

In a room with a high ceiling, the ceiling is often the room's dominant visual element. Uplighting the ceiling—which can be done in a variety of ways—emphasizes it.

One approach is to place uplight wall sconces around the room where the architecture permits. Fixtures with 150-watt halogen bulbs are good in a large room. Set the fixtures above eye level and at least 3 feet from the ceiling. Fixtures can be as far as 10 feet apart on a long wall, but for even light on the ceiling, space them no more than twice their distance from the ceiling.

Uplight chandeliers mounted at least 8 feet above the floor and at least 3 feet from the ceiling will also highlight the ceiling. A single fixture of 300 watts will cover about 300 square feet.

If beams span the room, you can install lights on top of them or on the sides. Incandescent wall sconces work well; floodlights will give a high-tech effect. Space the lights evenly, about 8 feet apart. For a brighter effect conceal two-tube fluorescent strip lights on the beams, adding a 3½-inch wooden fascia to hide the fixtures. Butt 48-inch fixtures together, end to end, and do not mix fixtures of different lengths.

Torchères—standing lamps that distribute light upward—offer a simple way to light a ceiling. Most torchères use 150- to 300-watt halogen bulbs; many have integral dimmers or high-low settings. Some models have cooler-operating compact fluorescent lamps; these are good choices where children are present. You can place a portable torchère wherever you have a convenient wall receptacle.

CONTROLS

Control each layer of lighting separately. Preset or digital dimmers allow more flexibility when adjusting the light in the room and make it easy to turn them on to the same level every time. It's easy to adjust the intensity of a high-wattage table lamp with a cord-and-plug dimmer. Provide a three-way control for a large room or one with multiple entries. Combine the controls in a common wall box to improve its appearance.

Multiscene dimming systems link several dimmers together so you can adjust all the lights simultaneously. They also let you create push-button presets for different activities, such as reading, conversation, or watching television. Hardwired dimming systems are used in new construction, but power line carrier devices (which transmit signals through the house's electrical wiring) and wireless systems are relatively easy to retrofit.

LIVING ROOM LIGHTING PLAN

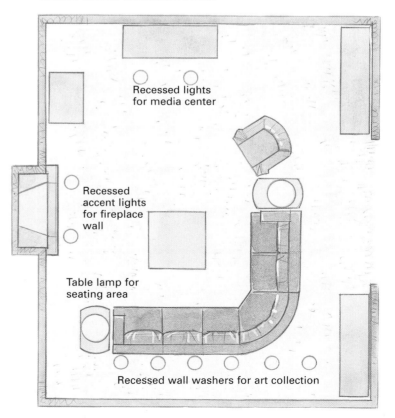

Recessed lights for media center

Recessed accent lights for fireplace wall

Table lamp for seating area

Recessed wall washers for art collection

THE BEDROOM

Cove lighting above the headboard and bedside lamps make this bedroom comfortable and relaxing. Added ambient light comes from a ceiling fixture when needed.

Most bedrooms have a switch by the door to control either a central overhead fixture or a receptacle for a table lamp. The primary consideration in lighting your bedroom is providing good light for dressing and reading while maximizing comfort.

LIGHTING IN CLOSETS

Good lighting helps you distinguish blue socks from black, match two shades of red, or find a pair of shoes in the back of the closet. Place a ceiling light in the center of a deep closet or just above the door in a shallow one. Clothing and shelves often block the light; several fixtures may be necessary to light the closet thoroughly. Use incandescent lights or fluorescent sources with good color rendition. Both have limitations: Fluorescent light dulls reds and oranges; incandescent light dulls blues.

Incandescent fixtures in a closet must be fully enclosed, according to the National Electrical Code (NEC). Surface-mounted incandescent fixtures must be 12 inches from the edge of any shelf or hanging area. Fluorescent fixtures, which can be unenclosed, must be 6 inches from a shelf. Pendant fixtures are not allowed by the NEC.

Local codes may have other limitations.

If you do not have room for lights in the closet, place recessed fixtures in front of it. Be sure they are far enough from the bed that you do not look up into them when you are lying down.

Turn closet lights on and off with a wall switch or a doorjamb switch, which turns lights on when the door opens and turns them off when it closes. Some closet lights have a pull-chain switch or include a knock-out so you can wire one in.

READING IN BED

Stand a short reading lamp on a table beside the bed, attach one to the headboard, or fasten it to the wall. A translucent shade helps illuminate the room but may bother the person next to you who is trying to sleep. An opaque shade blocks stray light. Swing-arm lamps are easy to move into the most comfortable position for reading. Plug reading lamps into unswitched receptacles so you do not have to get out of bed to turn them off.

AMBIENT LIGHT

Ambient light illuminates the room for dressing, cleaning, and simply moving about. A central, decorative fixture with two or three 60-watt bulbs is usually adequate. Choose one that's not too big or too small for the room. An uplight is a good choice in a room with a 10-foot ceiling.

If you install a ceiling fan in the bedroom, add a light kit. It will not deliver as much light as a ceiling fixture, but will dispel shadows. A single, bottom light kit with a diffusing shade is better than a ring of small lamps, which tend to glare. A 52-inch fan works well in a 15×15-foot bedroom.

A round fluorescent fixture is a good choice for a child's bedroom. It gives more light for playing on the floor or cleaning up. And the long life and low energy cost pay off when the light is on for a long time. Choose one that has two circular or three compact fluorescent lamps and is designed for a slightly larger room.

If you have a desk, vanity, or reading chair, provide a lamp for it. A diffusing shade creates a more pleasing glow than overhead lighting. If the lamp provides primary ambient light for the room, plug it into a receptacle controlled by a switch at the door.

Control the ceiling fixture with a dimmer so you can reduce the lighting at night; brighten it while getting dressed in the morning.

Wall sconces

Table lamp for reading

Wall-mounted reading lamp

BEDROOM LIGHTING PLAN

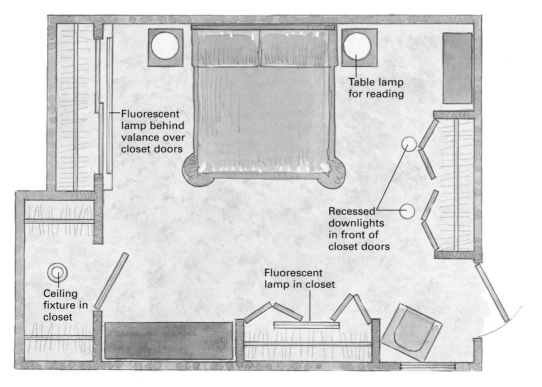

Table lamp for reading

Fluorescent lamp behind valance over closet doors

Recessed downlights in front of closet doors

Ceiling fixture in closet

Fluorescent lamp in closet

THE BATHROOM

Sconces are mounted on the mirror in this master bath. Mounting the fixtures high above eye level hides reflections of their interiors and prevents glare.

B athroom lighting depends on who is using the room: adults or children, homeowners or guests. A master bath needs good light for grooming in comfort and style. Children's bathrooms need bright lighting and simple fixtures. Lighting in the guest bath or powder room is selected more for the style and appearance of the fixtures than for their effectiveness. The layers of light in a bathroom include light at the mirror for grooming; lights for the shower, spa, or a separate toilet; and ambient lighting.

MAINTENANCE

Bathroom lights are among the most used in the home. Expect to change an incandescent bulb at least once a year. Relamping an enclosed fixture may involve loosening hard-to-reach thumbscrews or removing metal shrouds, which may be difficult for older people. If this is an issue, look for a fixture with easy-to-remove diffusers. Because of their short lamp life and low efficiency, incandescent sources cost six to seven times as much to operate as fluorescent.

Recessed lights in a soffit over the sinks and a large wall-mounted fixture in the shower stall fill this contemporary bathroom with light.

GOOD LIGHT FOR GROOMING

Light for grooming must surround the face, eliminating the natural shadows under the eyebrows, nose, and chin. It must be bright enough to put on makeup, yet be comfortable. Bathroom light should reveal—and flatter—skin tones.

LOCATING THE LIGHTS: To direct light all around your face, locate a 24- or 36-inch vertical bracket light on either side of the mirror. Center the brackets 66 inches above the floor. Longer fixtures put out more light and spread it better, even reaching under the chin.

If the bathroom arrangement does not permit side lighting, locate a single fixture over the mirror, 78 inches above the floor. Install the longest fixture that will fit, one at least 24 inches long.

If you are selecting a new fixture to replace one mounted over the mirror, get the longest one that will fit. Spread the light out over the fixture: Three 75-watt bulbs are better than two 100-watt bulbs, although the light output is about the same.

CHOOSING THE LIGHT SOURCE: Bath fixtures are available with incandescent, halogen, or fluorescent bulbs. Incandescent A lamps are inexpensive and easy to replace. Enclosed fixtures that use them are usually limited in wattage, however, due to heat and size. Incandescent G lamps are common in the least expensive fixtures, but their light is very yellow. Fixtures with halogen bulbs provide whiter, brighter light. They generate a lot of heat in a small space. Replacement bulbs are often expensive too.

Fluorescent light offers several advantages. The light is diffused along the length of the tube, which is more comfortable. For the same amount of light, fluorescent sources create about one-fourth the heat of incandescent bulbs, so you do not get as hot when close to the mirror. Light output is high, as well. A 3-foot fixture with two 25-watt T8 tubes delivers nearly twice as much light as a bare-lamp bath strip. The brightness of fluorescent lighting makes it a good choice in a children's bath. Use no. 830 tubes, which have a better color balance than G lamps (especially for older eyes). The challenge with fluorescent lighting may be finding a fixture in the style you want.

CHOOSING THE FIXTURE: For the most comfortable lighting, look for thickly etched, sandblasted, or white opal glass diffusers. Light from the ordinary bare-lamp makeup-mirror bar is harsh. Some bath fixtures can be placed either vertically or horizontally; others only mount one way. Check before you purchase. Get a fluorescent fixture with an electronic ballast.

Many materials and finishes—ceramic tile, chrome plumbing fixtures, or wooden cabinets—compete for attention in most bathrooms. Unless you want the lighting to be the prominent element in the design, choose a simple, understated fixture style that blends in.

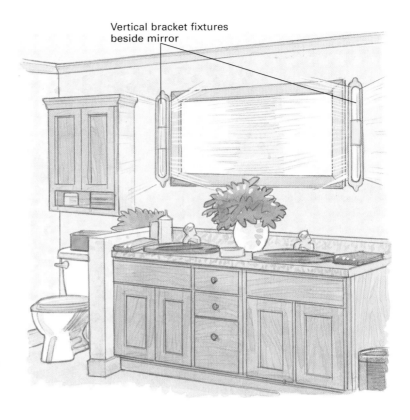

Vertical bracket fixtures beside mirror

In a powder room where appearance is what counts, sconces, swagged mini-pendants, or other stylish fixtures contribute to the decor. Because these bathrooms are intended for brief use by short-term guests, lighting performance is secondary to style.

Downlights placed over sides of sinks minimize face shadows.

THE BATHROOM
continued

An arch built in front of the mirror wall conceals strip lights, which light the mirror and add a decorative glow.

A pendant fixture, bracket lights flanking the mirror, and small display-cabinet downlights brighten the bathroom above. The guest powder room (right) uses halogen wall brackets.

DOWNLIGHTS OVER THE SINK

A downlight installed directly over the sink—often as a simple lighting solution—casts strong shadows. To minimize the problem, locate downlights on each side of the sink instead of putting one directly above it. Place 5- or 7-inch fixtures with 60- or 75-watt A lamps as close to the mirror as is comfortable. Set the fixtures so the bulbs are well above the ceiling for the best light.

BUILT-IN FLUORESCENT LIGHTING

One way to avoid style and appearance problems with fluorescent lighting is to build it into a concealed pocket over the mirror. This is most practical if you are building a home or addition or remodeling a bathroom. Because this kind of lighting depends on

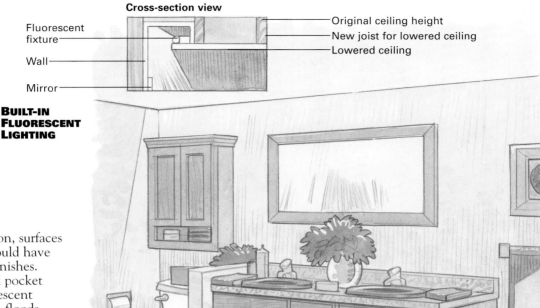

Cross-section view

Fluorescent fixture

Wall

Mirror

Original ceiling height
New joist for lowered ceiling
Lowered ceiling

BUILT-IN FLUORESCENT LIGHTING

surface reflection, surfaces in the bath should have light-colored finishes. The completed pocket hides the fluorescent lighting, which floods the room and illuminates faces comfortably.

Concealed lighting requires a pocket 6 to 12 inches deep above the mirror. This may require lowering the ceiling in all or part of the room. Leave a 6-inch opening along the mirror and provide a ledge for mounting fluorescent strip lights. The top of the mirror should be 12 inches below the ceiling opening to ensure that the fixtures will not reflect in the mirror. Finish the wall inside the pocket all the way to the top of the pocket to match the rest of the walls.

Install narrow, one-tube strip lights, staggering them in an over/under arrangement so they completely fill the pocket. Use strips of the same length.

LIGHTING A SHOWER

Most shower lights are recessed fixtures with a glass or plastic diffuser with gaskets. They fit standard recessed housings. If you choose glass, look for a fixture with a retaining bale to hold the diffuser while you relamp the fixture—the bail prevents dropping the breakable glass diffuser in the shower. A shower that has a transparent curtain or door may not need a separate light.

LIGHTING A SPA

A spa or whirlpool contains a motor that creates the water jets. Because of this the National Electric Code requires special construction for any lighting within 7 feet of the water line or 2 feet of the edge of the tub. Spa-rated fixtures must be suitable for installation in a wet location and have no exposed metal parts. Manufacturers generally mark such fixtures clearly. Track lighting is not approved for use in either damp or wet locations, even beyond the 7-foot limits.

AMBIENT LIGHTING

If the bathroom is large or has a freestanding sink (not a vanity), a separate toilet stall, or dark finishes, additional ambient light will be necessary. Ceiling, wall, or recessed fixtures (with A or flood bulbs) are good choices. Choose fixtures in scale with the room.

CONTROLS

Control mirror, shower, and toilet lighting separately so you only use the lights you need. Install a dimmer for incandescent mirror lighting. This allows you to provide a dimmed night-light or to turn lights to low intensity when using the bathroom in the middle of the night.

THE HOME OFFICE AND WORKROOM

A computer is likely to be the center of a home office. Like television, the computer is self-luminous; you do not need additional light to view the screen. In fact, light falling on the screen usually obscures the image. Much of the time spent in an office with a computer, however, also involves looking at printed materials. The key to lighting the computerized home office is lighting the desk area without washing out the display screen. You also need to provide light around the room so you can find books, do filing, and use other equipment, such as a calculator.

TASK LIGHTING

Desk lamps make good task lights because you can position them so they don't shine on the screen. A high-intensity lamp casts a well-defined beam but adds little to the ambient brightness. A translucent shade creates a warmer atmosphere. To avoid shadows when writing, locate the lamp to the left side of the desk if you are right-handed (and opposite for lefties). Older adults need much more light than children. A 100-watt incandescent or 18-watt compact fluorescent bulb will work fine in a youngster's lamp. But an older person

A fluorescent fixture mounted on the bottom of the overhead cabinet provides plenty of light for this quilter's worktable.

might need a lamp with a 200-watt bulb. A three-position switch and a three-way bulb or a lamp dimmer increase flexibility.

Ceiling-mounted lighting causes problems when it reflects onto the computer screen. Uplights (pendants, close-to-ceiling, or fan kits) work best because they spread light across the ceiling. Downlights will be comfortable as long as they are located to the sides of the room and not directly over the computer area (or your chair).

AMBIENT LIGHTING

Unless you spend your day doing intensive, graphics-oriented work on your computer, you will probably find a dark office uncomfortable. Use ambient lighting to balance the brightness of the desk and computer screen and to lighten the space. You can use overhead lighting, provided you control the screen reflections. If your task area is well-lighted, you will not need more than two watts per square foot of incandescent lighting.

If you work more than a couple of hours at a time in your home office, you may prefer fluorescent lighting. It provides a broader wash, adds less heat to the room, and gives more illumination. Use a ceiling fixture or a compact fluorescent torchère. Ask your lighting dealer about special-ordering a fluorescent pendant; they are now common in commercial installations. Or, mount strip lights behind a valance on the wall or on the top of bookcases to provide indirect lighting. (see page 56.)

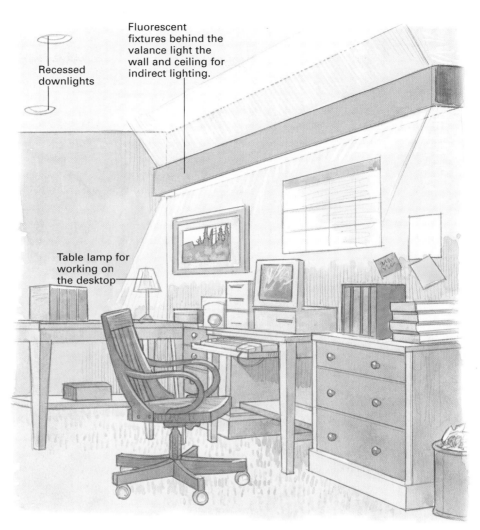

Recessed downlights

Fluorescent fixtures behind the valance light the wall and ceiling for indirect lighting.

Table lamp for working on the desktop

you can work on projects that need a lot of light. Fluorescent lighting provides the most economical solution, especially if you move from room to room, leaving the lights on until you return.

A large ceiling-mounted fluorescent fixture will provide the necessary light if you allow two tubes for every 60 square feet of space. Even in utility spaces, it feels better to have type 830 tubes for good color rendition.

Locate fluorescent task lights on the underside of shelves over a work surface so you will not be working in your own shadow.

THE WORKROOM

Laundry and utility rooms require lighting for manual—rather than paper—tasks. High levels of diffused light enable you to see into washers and dryers and to perform small repairs. It is also convenient to have one brightly lighted room in the house where

CONTROLS

Control incandescent ambient lighting with a dimmer to adjust intensity and prolong the life of the bulbs. If you work full time at home, install a dimmer for fluorescent ambient lighting so you can set the best light level in the office for your work.

LESSENING LIGHT POLLUTION

Well-planned and carefully installed outdoor lighting enhances the landscape, improves visibility, and increases safety and security. But careless use of lights outside simply adds to light pollution.

Light pollution is light that serves no purpose. Usually it escapes from landscape lighting or outdoor safety and security lighting. Effects range from annoying, such as light that shines into the bedroom from a neighbor's yard or washes out the view of stars in the night sky, to dangerous, like glare that distracts or temporarily blinds a passing motorist. Light pollution also represents wasted energy and money.

The recommendations in this chapter will help you avoid light pollution. Keep these general principles in mind as you plan and install outdoor lighting.

AIM LIGHTS CAREFULLY: A beam or wash of light on a shrub is a great accent, but some of the light from a poorly aimed lamp can shine past the bush, possibly into someone's window. Aim lights at night, and check them frequently in case lawnmowing or gardening jars them out of position.

SHIELD BULBS: Stray light increases light pollution and diminishes the effect of your outdoor lighting. Use fixtures that have reflectors and shielding to reduce glare and concentrate the light where you want it. Install lights behind or below natural shields when possible.

MINIMIZE WATTAGE: You can see outside at night with just a little light; low-wattage bulbs usually provide ample illumination. Higher wattage often makes the light harsher without improving the aesthetic effect of the lighting or increasing safety or security.

CONTROL THE LIGHT: Install the lights in separately controllable zones with timers, photo controls, or motion sensors so lights are on only when needed. Dimmers help match the light to the environment.

LIGHTING IN THE NIGHT ENVIRONMENT

You can see better with less light outdoors at night than you can indoors. That's because your eyes adapt to nighttime darkness and become more sensitive to even the slightest

contrast between a dimly lighted object and the dark background. Light and shadow create recognizable patterns too.

Outdoors at night a little light can accomplish a lot. Most outdoor surfaces are dark and do not reflect light well, so outdoor lighting depends on direct illumination rather than bounce or fill light. Fixtures must be located to put the light exactly where you want it. At the same time they must be positioned and shielded to prevent glare.

When you plan outdoor lighting, walk around your yard at night and imagine the lighting effects you want. As your eyes adapt to the darkness, you will appreciate the power of just a little light.

Fixtures mounted on the exterior walls of your home can be connected to house wiring, but you will have to bring power to landscape lighting fixtures. Low-voltage systems make this a practical do-it-yourself project in many cases. An electrician or landscape contractor can give you advice about extending electrical lines for line-voltage outdoor lighting.

It doesn't take a lot of light to make your yard look magical at night. Downlights in these trees illuminate the path and accent the trees themselves. Accent lighting dramatizes the view of the house.

PATHWAYS

A well-lighted entry path extends hospitality to family and guests and enhances safety and security. Steps, in particular, need even illumination. Warm light on faces at the front door makes it easy to identify visitors. People feel most secure when lighting eliminates shadows that might conceal an intruder.

FRONT ENTRY LIGHTING

Security light with motion sensor   Wall brackets at front entry   Downlight for driveway and entry

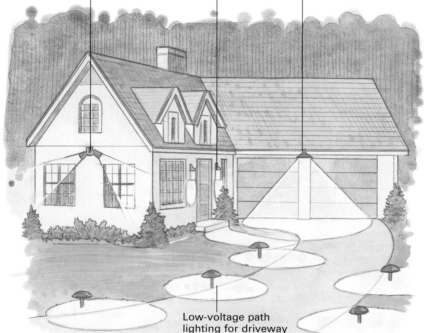

Low-voltage path lighting for driveway

LOW-VOLTAGE PATH LIGHT

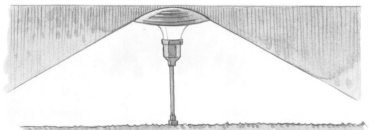

LOW-VOLTAGE GARDEN LIGHT

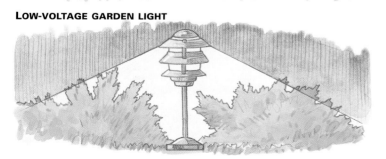

FRONT ENTRY

Wall-mounted or pendant lanterns are good fixtures for front-entry lighting. Locate the lights where they look best on the house. Align wall brackets that flank the entry with architectural details, such as window frames, and make sure hanging fixtures clear the door swing. Put clear bulbs into clear glass lanterns, frosted bulbs into translucent glass. Entry lights don't need to be bright; 40- to 75-watt bulbs work fine. Light a large entry with several fixtures, rather than one with higher-wattage bulbs that adds little spread and makes the entry fixtures glare. You can supplement wall or hanging fixtures with downlights, but do not rely on them alone; they cast unflattering shadows on faces.

PATHWAYS

Downlight paths with low path lights or floodlights mounted in trees. Lights in trees create a wide, bright walkway and dispel shadows in nearby shrubs. Low-level path lights illuminate the walk, but leave shrubbery in shadow, keeping the focus on the lighted entry. Tree-mounted lighting, whether line-voltage or low-voltage, is more difficult to install and maintain. If you have a detached garage, light the path or breezeway between it and the house.

DRIVEWAY

Light a driveway 100 feet long or shorter with low-voltage garden lights or louvered path lights. The effect will not be as bright as 120-volt lights, but the installation is easier. Mount the transformer at the house and run cables down either side of the driveway. You can attach an accent light to illuminate a sign with your street number or name. Locate the light within two feet of the sign and aim it up to the sign at a steep angle. The fixture should be well-shielded (add a cowl if needed) so light won't glare in your eyes as you drive out to the street.

For decorative effect, line the driveway with low-voltage path lights. You can mount spotlights with PAR lamps in trees to illuminate the pavement, following the guidelines on the opposite page.

To light a basketball court or other paved area beside the house, mount lights on the side of the house or garage, about 10 feet above the ground. You can use PAR lamps in simple utility brackets or an HID wall pack. Shield the lights and aim them down. Check local building codes for regulations on light pollution because this type of area lighting is often visible from neighboring property or public streets.

LOW-LEVEL PATH LIGHTING

Low-voltage fixtures mounted on short stems are effective for path lighting. Depending on the design, they may direct all the light down (mushroom style) or broadcast some light to create miniature beacons that mark the path (bollard, louvered, or pagoda style).

To make a nearly continuous ribbon of light along the path, follow the manufacturer's spacing recommendations. You can usually space mushrooms 8 to 12 feet apart, depending on the size of the fixture and the height of the stem. Space pagoda-style fixtures a little closer together. To create discreet pools of light along the path for atmospheric effect, space the lights farther apart. Tree-mounted downlights will also make light pools; keep the intensity low by using 20-watt bulbs.

PAVERS

Mark the edges of a brick walkway with in-ground, low-voltage pavers. These luminous fixtures replace individual bricks in the path. They do not illuminate the path itself, but simply indicate its direction or mark the boundary. (See photo, page 78.)

STEPS

Steps or any part of a path that abruptly changes height must be lighted clearly for safety. Recess step lights into an adjacent wall or post to sweep stair treads with light. The higher you mount the step light, the larger the area it will illuminate. A step light mounted 2 feet above the step will usually throw light 3 to 4 feet. Installing step lights in masonry or where line-voltage power is not available is probably a job for a professional electrician.

TREE-MOUNTED LIGHTS

A floodlight mounted in a tree will illuminate an area about the same diameter as the mounting height. A light mounted 15 feet above the ground will light an area about 15 feet across, for example. Place the lights so they cover the entire path, especially the ends and any steps. Use a fixture that shields the light source or that can be fitted with an accessory shroud or cowl. Bulbs can be flood (FL) or wide flood (WFL) type. For tree-mounting, install high-quality bulbs for long lamp life. Attach fixtures and cable to the tree with stainless-steel fasteners.

MUSHROOM LIGHTS

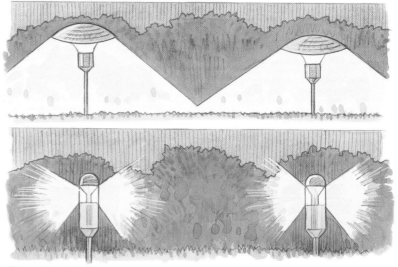

BOLLARD LIGHTS

CONTROLS

Control path and entry lighting with a timer, photocell, or a conventional switch or dimmer. The timer turns lights on and off at fixed times, which you can set. Some timers permit two on-off cycles per day. A photocell turns lights on when darkness falls and off when daylight returns. Transformers for low-voltage lighting are usually available with a built-in control option. Photocells and timer switches can be wired to a 120-volt circuit in an outlet or switch box. Security lights with motion sensors turn on when anything moves in the target area.

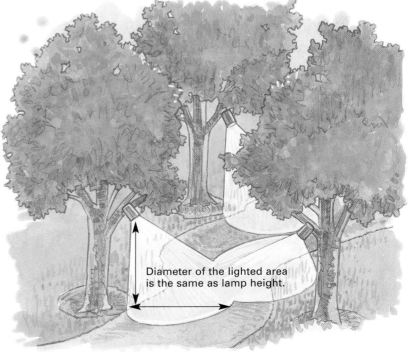

Diameter of the lighted area is the same as lamp height.

PATIOS

Lighting a deck or patio expands your living area and increases your enjoyment of it. At night you can see the patio or deck better from inside the house because the lighting overcomes the mirror effect of looking out a window from a bright interior.

On a patio the easiest way to light people's faces is to place candles or battery-powered camping lanterns on a table or low parapet. Low-intensity light reflecting off a surface creates an intimate social area. Lighting the patio surface makes the outdoor space more relaxed and comfortable. Downlights directed at a grill or cooking area make it easier to prepare food after dark. Patio lighting is mostly low-voltage, so some of the techniques for path lighting apply to deck and patio lighting as well.

Lighted pavers are ideal for marking the edges of patios or paths. Add supplemental downlights to illuminate the surface.

DECK LIGHTS

Deck lights—small low-voltage fixtures—mount on posts, walls, or other surfaces, such as the edges of benches. They wash the deck or patio surface, illuminating and defining the area. Deck lights are usually hooded to shield the light source and reduce glare.

For widest coverage mount deck lights just below seated eye level, about 24 to 36 inches above the deck or patio surface, depending on the height of your deck furniture. Check the viewing angles from the lower levels of multilevel decks to be sure lights will not glare in the eyes of people seated there. Lights spaced up to 6 feet apart generally provide an even light wash around the edge of the deck.

Hide the pigtail connection from the deck light to the low-voltage cable. For a light mounted on a post, drill down through the post from the mounting height with a spade bit and extensions, angling downward so the hole exits on the back side at the base of the post. You can then run the pigtail under the deck and splice it to the cable. (See pages 82–85 for information about installing low-voltage systems.)

If your brick patio is not walled or fenced in, you can delineate it with in-ground pavers spaced around the edges. (See photo above.)

DECK AND PATIO LIGHTS

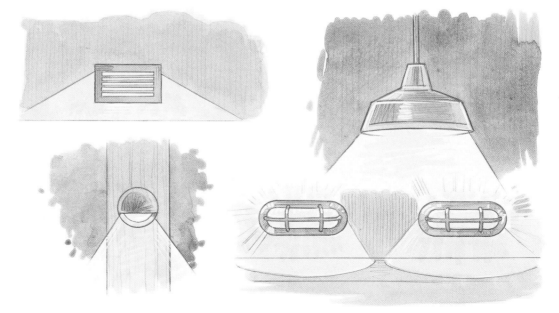

Deck lights on wall

Portable fixture for table lighting

DOWNLIGHTS

Low-intensity downlighting from a tree, a roof overhang, or a yard structure lights a deck or patio softly. The glow of the light itself adds visual interest as well. Use small, low-voltage pendants, either solid or perforated, that completely shield a low-wattage light source. Avoid bright lights so your patio won't be lit up like a ballpark.

GRILL OR BARBEQUE

If your grill is near the house, mount line-voltage cylinder downlights on the wall to illuminate the cooking area. A downlight with a flood bulb mounted 8 feet above the deck will illuminate an area extending 3 to 5 feet from the house. Use a deep cylinder and short-neck PAR30 bulb to avoid glare. You can also use decorative fixtures with bulbs no larger than 60 watts. They will appear bright in the dark but the light will not carry very far, so you may want to supplement the light with a portable lantern.

   If the grill is farther away from the house, downlight the area with low-voltage lights.

CONTROLS

Low-voltage transformers usually plug into an outdoor outlet near the area they are lighting. Wire the outlet to a switch near the patio door so you can control the lights conveniently. (See pages 82–85 for information about installing low-voltage lighting and dimming transformers.)

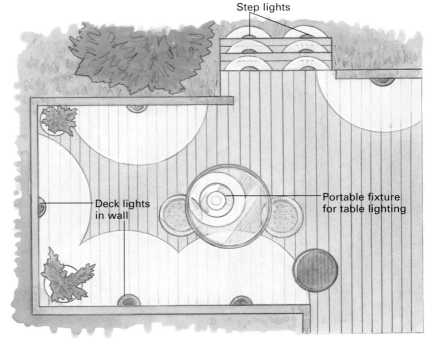

Step lights

Deck lights in wall

Portable fixture for table lighting

GARDENS

A beautifully illuminated garden or landscape enhances the beauty of your home whether viewed from the garden, the street, or inside your home. Rather than the more functional patio or pathway lighting, the lighting of trees, shrubs, flower beds, and garden sculpture provides aesthetic enjoyment just as accent lighting enhances indoor living spaces.

Most landscape lighting uses low-voltage accent lights that shine onto foliage or low-level garden lights that illuminate the plantings beneath them. The two considerations for pleasing effects are:

■ Shield the light sources so they are not visible.

■ Do not overpower the foliage with too much light. Use wide beam light sources to avoid hotspots, which look unnatural.

A fixture shields the bulb to prevent glare.

BE SELECTIVE

It is neither practical nor desirable to light your entire property; you must be selective. First consider the best views of the landscape from the house and yard. Next choose the features that will look most interesting when illuminated. These may be large trees, shrubbery or flowers, walls, or sculpture. Then compose a lighted scene with these elements, identifying the visual focus. Finally determine how you want to light each element (there may be just one, of course) for the best effect.

TREES

The broad canopy of a tree's branches looks most attractive cross-lighted from the ground with two or three accent lights. Use deep, well-shielded fixtures; add a shroud or cowl if needed. Keep light levels low; 20- to 35-watt low-voltage MR or PAR flood lamps provide enough light for all but the largest trees.

To position the lamps, determine the distance from the ground to the bottom of the lowest branches, or those that form most of the canopy. Put the lamps about half that distance from the tree trunk, and aim them up about 60 degrees. Keep the lights away from low plants with leaves that might block some of the light. Adjust the lamps so the light illuminates the leaves and branches low in the canopy but doesn't escape past the tree.

SHRUBBERY

Large bushes and shrubs often present interesting textures and outlines. To highlight shrubbery, place accent lights 3 feet away. A single fixture will cover a plant about 3 feet wide. Use 20-watt MR16 flood lamps. If the shrubs grow in front of a wall, the light will create intriguing shadow patterns on it.

Silhouette shrubbery by lighting a vertical surface behind it. This technique, also called backlighting, leaves the front of the plant in shadow and emphasizes its outline.

LOW PLANTINGS

Downlight flower beds and other low plantings with small garden or path lights on short stems. To evenly light a narrow area of planting, or the edge of a larger bed, use the path lighting technique shown on page 77. Separate the fixtures to create pools of light.

VERTICAL SURFACES

Textured surfaces such as fieldstone walls stand out when they are lit at a raking angle. Mount accent lights about 12 inches from the base of the wall and aim them up the wall, keeping the light on the wall. Space the lamps about 18 inches apart. Use 20-watt MR flood lamps and add an accessory shade, if needed, to prevent light from glaring into people's eyes.

Light illuminates the tree, but does not escape into the sky.

Cross-light tree with two or three fixtures on the ground.

BACKLIGHTING A SHRUB

HIGHLIGHTING A SHRUB

STATUES

Highlight a statue by placing an accent light 45 degrees to one side of it, aiming up from the ground. Make the distance from the base to the lamp the same as the height from the ground to the midpoint of the statue (including the base). Aim the lamp so the beam isn't visible from viewing angles and doesn't shine into windows. A 20-watt bulb—flood or spot, depending on the object's size—is adequate for most objects. Even with low light, a statue stands out from the landscape because it is reflective.

POOLS AND SPAS

Light shimmering on water creates a magical effect, but be careful when using electricity near or in water. Any equipment installed in water should be clearly marked for underwater use. (Some low-voltage pool lights are shown on page 84.) Buy built-in, line-voltage pool lighting, especially, from a qualified dealer, and have it installed by a professional.

Light the patio areas adjacent to a pool with path lights or pavers. Keep them 10 feet from the edge of the water. These provide decorative light for socializing, but not safety or security lighting for the pool. Downlights and accent lights installed in nearby trees can provide light on the surface of the pool. Fiber optic systems are ideal for ponds and pools. (See the sidebar at right.)

CONTROLS

Control garden lighting with timer or photocell controls described on page 77.

FIBER-OPTIC LIGHTING

Fiber-optic systems distribute light from a light source, called the *illuminator*, through plastic cable, to various light-emitting components. Fiber optics are popular for ponds and pools because the electric connection to the illuminator can be located away from the water. The single light source also simplifies maintenance. Only the illuminator requires an electrical connection; the rest of the system is nonelectrified. Light emitters in a fiber-optic system remain cool to the touch.

Fiber-optic cables are connected to the illuminator with special fittings and are usually cut to length during installation. A single illuminator can drive multiple cables or a single loop of luminous cable. Fiber-optic illuminators use low-voltage halogen sources for smaller systems or metal halide sources for larger installations.

Fiber-optic underwater fittings and connections can be used inside the pool. Or you can have the edge of the pool outlined by luminous cable. An optional rotating color wheel inside the illuminator changes the color of the light.

As with low-voltage lighting systems, fiber-optic systems consist of numerous components, all of which must work together correctly to be effective. A special tool is required to cut the fiber-optic cable and preserve its light-conveying properties. Kits with matched components are available for do-it-yourself installation. Consult a professional for large projects.

INSTALLING LOW-VOLTAGE LIGHTING

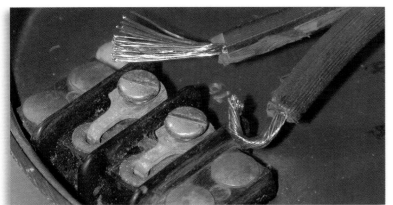

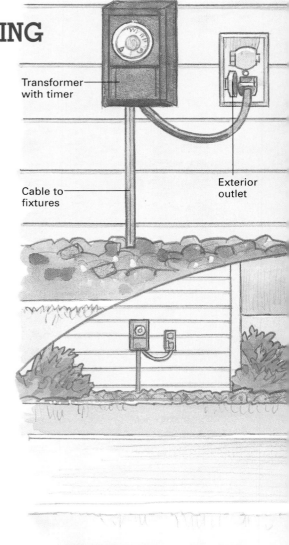

Transformer with timer

Cable to fixtures

Exterior outlet

Low-voltage cable usually connects to the transformer at screw terminals. Strip the cable, twist the stranded conductors together, then form a loop to hook around the screw.

Low-voltage landscape lighting systems operate at 12 volts. The complete system includes a transformer, low-voltage cable, fixtures, and accessories. Components are available separately or in ready-to-install kits. You can install most basic low-voltage landscape lighting yourself.

TRANSFORMER

A transformer receives 120-volt power at the input (called the transformer's *primary side*) and reduces it to 12 volts at the output terminals (called the *secondary side*). The primary connections are fully enclosed for safety. Most residential transformers connect to the line-voltage source with a standard cord and plug. The secondary connections are exposed—usually screw terminals— for installing the cable. Coming into contact with connectors or bare wires on the low-voltage side of the system is not hazardous.

Choose a transformer according to the load—the wattage of all the lights you will operate from the transformer. The load should be within 50 to 80 percent of the rated capacity of the transformer. For example use a 300-watt transformer for 150- to 240- watt loads. While most transformers operate safely up to their maximum rated capacity, allow at least 20 percent more capacity in case you add lights later. Transformers usually have circuit breakers for overload protection. A transformer that's too large for the load may overdrive the lamps, shortening their life spans.

Transformers can mount to the side of the home, at least 12 inches above the ground. The power cord plugs into an outdoor receptacle. Most transformers are rated for use in wet outdoor locations. If you install the transformer in the garage, find a model rated for indoor use.

LOW-VOLTAGE CABLE

Landscape lighting cable looks like heavy lamp cord, with two stranded conductors (Type SPT-3). Larger-diameter conductors (designated by smaller gauge numbers) can carry more current. (See "Voltage Drop" on the opposite page.) Use 14-gauge cable for short runs,12-gauge for longer ones. Cable comes in various lengths, and is easy to cut or splice. The cable is the least expensive part of the system, so don't scrimp.

Cable does not need to be fully entrenched; it can be concealed by mulch or another ground covering. Where cable would be exposed to lawn or garden maintenance, however, bury it 4 inches below ground to avoid damage.

FIXTURES AND ACCESSORIES

Pigtail leads on lighting fixtures attach to the main cable. Some fixtures have leads with easy-to-use, press-on connectors. These have

Fixtures

metal teeth that pierce the cable covering and make electrical contact with the wires inside, eliminating the need for stripping wires and splicing them. To attach these connectors, open the body, slip it over the cable, then press the connector closed. If the fixture does not have a connector, splice the leads to the cable as described on page 85.

Better accent lights have an extended housing that shields the lamp from view. An accessory cowl or shroud—which does the same thing—can be added to many lamps.

Fixtures that don't come with a mounting stake usually attach to an accessory stake or stem, which is purchased separately. To assemble the fixture to its mounting device, first run the lead wires out the bottom, then thread the device to the fixture.

VOLTAGE DROP

Voltage decreases as electricity travels along low-voltage cable. The amount of voltage drop depends on the gauge of the wire, the length of the cable, and the load connected to it. As voltage drops, light output diminishes (and lamp life increases). If there is too much drop, fixtures at the end of the cable may not provide as much light as you want and there will be less quantity and color of light than that of fixtures closer to the transformer (where the drop is less).

Keep voltage drop below 8 to 10 percent (1 to 1.3 volts) for the best results. You can usually run 12-gauge cable up to 100 feet without excessive voltage drop, providing you keep the total load under 100 watts.

To calculate the drop in volts, use the following formula and accompanying table:

Voltage drop = [Total watts on cable × Cable length]/Cable constant

Cable Constant			
Cable size:	16 gauge	14 gauge	12 gauge	10 gauge
Constant:	2,200	3,500	7,500	11,920

For example, here's how to calculate the voltage drop for a circuit that has five fixtures with 20-watt bulbs attached to 100 feet of 12-2 cable:

Total watts on cable = 5 fixtures × 20 watts = 100 watts
100 watts × 100 (Cable length) = 10,000
10,000/7,500 (Cable constant for 12-gauge cable) = 1.3 volts

To minimize voltage drop, divide the lighting up among several separate cables and run them all back to the transformer. You can also loop a single cable back to the transformer, connecting both ends to the terminal blocks, which halves its effective length. If you still need to handle a higher load or longer cable run, use 10-gauge cable, which reduces voltage drop by about 40 percent.

INSTALLING LOW-VOLTAGE LIGHTING
continued

Extend outdoor lighting to ponds or pools with low-voltage submersible fixtures. Clip-on color filters are available for many fixtures.

Attach fixtures to trees with screws or nails and secure the cable with nail-on clips. Tying or clamping around a tree's trunk or branches can harm the tree.

LAYING OUT THE SYSTEM

First sketch your lighting layout, keeping cable runs short to limit voltage drop. Next locate the fixtures following the placement guidelines on pages 76–81. Mark the locations clearly. Lay the cable on the ground, allowing enough extra length (about 3 feet) for burying or otherwise concealing it and for splicing. Extra cable also allows you to move fixtures as plants grow. Provide at least 10 feet of cable between the transformer and the first fixture to prevent overdriving the lamp.

ASSEMBLE AND INSTALL THE FIXTURES

Assemble and lamp the fixtures according to the manufacturer's directions. Seat the lamps securely in their sockets. High-heat silicone lubricant will protect the lamp contacts. Do not touch halogen bulbs with your bare fingers; the oil on your skin will shorten the life of the bulb. Accent fixtures often have

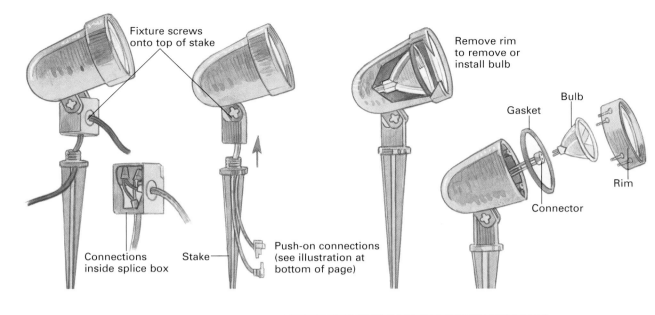

Fixture screws onto top of stake

Connections inside splice box

Stake

Push-on connections (see illustration at bottom of page)

Remove rim to remove or install bulb

Gasket

Bulb

Connector

Rim

a gasket between the body and lens; be sure it is intact. Apply a lubricant to the threads so you can easily remove the screws for relamping and cleaning. Leave the fixture leads exposed so you can attach them to the cable. Stake or fasten fixtures in place using stainless-steel fasteners for trees and stainless or brass hardware on a deck. For ground-mounted fixtures that must be spliced to the cable, mark the location but do not install the fixture. Then you can make the connections without stooping. Install the fixture after you finish the splicing.

CONNECTING THE SYSTEM

Low-voltage cable usually attaches to the transformer's secondary outputs at screw terminals. To connect the cable, strip the insulation back ¾ inch (or as specified by the transformer manufacturer), loosen the terminal screws, slide the leads in as recommended, and tighten securely.

Once the cable is attached, you can turn on the transformer and attach press-on fixtures to the cable while it is live, checking the connections as you go. The press-on connectors install without cutting the cable, which speeds up the project. Turn off the transformer, and cut the final end of the cable cleanly. Apply protective silicone gel and tape it for protection against moisture.

Leave the power off to make spliced connections because you need to cut the cable. On both ends of the cut cable, slice and separate the two leads for about 3 inches. Strip ¾ inch of insulation from each lead. Twist together a lead from the fixture and one lead from each end of the cable. Use gel-filled wire nuts to make the best connection.

CONTROLS

Plugging in and unplugging the transformer is the simplest way to control low-voltage outdoor lighting. For manual switch control, wire a switch to the receptacle that the transformer is plugged into. Locate the switch inside, near an entry, or outside in a weatherproof box in a convenient, sheltered location. Compatible low-voltage dimmers are available for many transformers. However you should hardwire the transformer to the dimmer using an exterior-rated junction box instead of plugging the power cord into a receptacle. For automatic control purchase a transformer with a built-in timer. Some transformers also accept a photocell accessory for daylight control.

PUSH-ON CONNECTOR

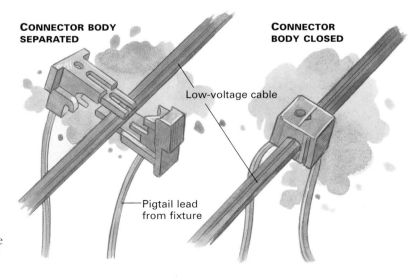

CONNECTOR BODY SEPARATED

CONNECTOR BODY CLOSED

Low-voltage cable

Pigtail lead from fixture

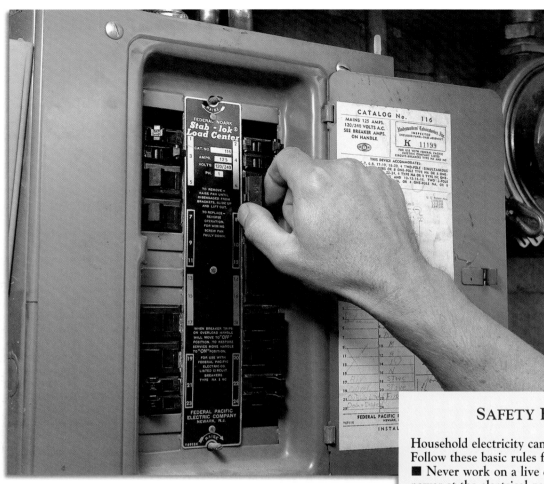

Before you do any electrical work in your house, find the circuit breaker panel. Always turn off the power to the circuit you're working on.

TOOLS AND SUPPLIES

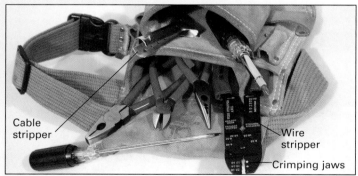

Cable stripper

Wire stripper

Crimping jaws

Use good tools; insulated rubber handles are a plus. If you will be working at the ceiling, get a sturdy ladder that has a shelf for tools and supplies. A tool belt or bucket will keep you from fumbling for your equipment. For most simple jobs, you will need screwdrivers—one with interchangeable bits and a long, thin one—as well as long-nose and lineman's pliers. If you are planning to run new wiring, add a wire stripper, a wire cutter, and a cable stripper or utility knife to your tool set. You'll need a drywall saw and a cordless drill to work with walls, ceilings, and wood framing. Supplies you'll need include wire nuts—suitable for no. 12 and 14 wire—and electrician's tape.

SAFETY FIRST

Household electricity can shock you. Follow these basic rules for safety:

■ Never work on a live circuit. Shut off the power at the electrical panel by turning off the circuit breaker. Post a sign or lock the panel box so no one accidentally restores power while you are working on the circuit.

■ Never touch the service wires that bring electricity into the panel. They are always live.

■ Turn off lights at the switch when replacing bulbs. Do not replace lamps in fixtures while they are on.

■ Wear gloves when adjusting the beams of accent lights; the fixtures get hot.

■ Do not work on a wet floor or with damp or greasy hands.

■ Work out your lighting and electrical plan in advance. Prepare a complete bill of material for all the fixtures, controls, and wiring supplies you will need. Have them all on hand before you start. For low-voltage systems and other products with many components, verify with your dealer that you have all the necessary parts.

■ Read and follow manufacturer's instructions and product labels for installation, use, and maintenance.

■ Installation tasks go faster and more safely when you have a helper.

INSTALLING LIGHTING EQUIPMENT

The cost and complexity of lighting installation depends on the scope of your project. Upgrading a fixture and replacing a switch with a dimmer are relatively easy jobs you can do yourself. Adding a new fixture with the associated wiring and controls is more challenging. The job is still within the do-it-yourself realm, but you may want to hire a qualified electrician. A building permit is often required for electrical wiring; check with your local building code authority. For more information about electrical work in your home, see Ortho's All About Wiring Basics.

The cost of electrical work increases substantially when the walls and ceiling are finished. If you are buying a new home or planning a major renovation, it's easier and more economical during construction to run wires and install boxes for all the lighting you want. Plan carefully; once the rough-in work is finished, changing the lighting layout becomes more expensive.

This section shows how the construction of your home affects your lighting options and explains basic installation techniques.

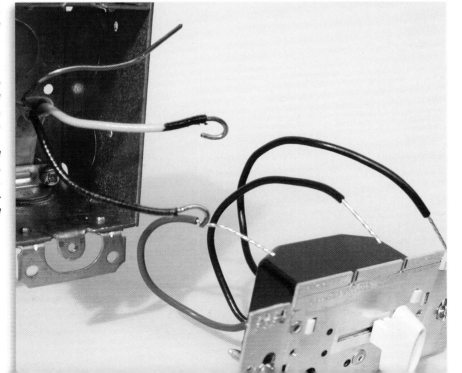

Most dimmers have pigtail connections. To install one in place of a switch with screw terminals, you'll need to snip the loops off the wires in the box. Here, you'll need to re-mark the white wire with black after cutting and stripping it.

ELECTRICITY

Even if you are just replacing a bathroom ceiling fixture, it helps to understand a little about electricity.

Current—the quantity or flow of electricity—is measured in amperes, or amps. The force that pushes the current is measured in volts. Power—the work that electricity performs—is measured in watts. The relation between current, voltage, and power is expressed by the formula: Watts = Volts × Amps.

Lightbulbs are rated by their power consumption in watts, an indirect way of comparing light output between bulbs. Divide watts by 120 (the voltage) to find how many amps a bulb uses. For example a 60-watt lightbulb uses ½ amp.

Electricity travels from the generating utility at high voltage. Transformers at utility substations and on power lines step the voltage down to household levels. Electricity at 120 volts enters your home through a service panel, which may be called a breaker box or panel or a load center. In the panel, the electrical service branches into separate circuits that deliver power to lighting and appliances throughout the home.

DO I HAVE ENOUGH ELECTRICAL SERVICE?

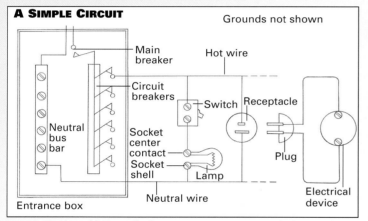

A SIMPLE CIRCUIT   Grounds not shown

Main breaker
Hot wire
Circuit breakers
Switch   Receptacle
Neutral bus bar
Socket center contact
Socket shell
Lamp
Plug
Electrical device
Entrance box
Neutral wire

Homes built today usually have 200 to 400 amps of electrical service, depending on the size of the home. This is ample for most needs. An older home, however, may lack adequate service for the lighting and appliances you want. Increasing the capacity of the electrical service is a job for a professional. Branches called circuits distribute electricity throughout the house.

There are three types of household circuits:
■ General-purpose circuits. These include lighting and receptacles. Lighting should be supplied by general-purpose circuits, which are usually 15 or 20 amps.
■ Small-appliance circuits. These supply receptacles in a specific area or use, such as the receptacles in the kitchen. A kitchen should have two 20-amp small-appliance circuits.
■ Individual circuits. These supply a single device, such as the range, washing machine, or dishwasher.

Even with adequate total service, branch circuits may not be enough for a lighting upgrade. Sophisticated lighting controls, in particular, require dedicated circuits. You can add branch circuits or rearrange existing circuits. But this is a job for a professional. If you are planning a major renovation, map your household circuits to determine how much electrical capacity you have available and where it is. You can do this by turning off the circuits one at a time and recording the loads connected to each. Plug in a lamp to check empty receptacles, which may not be on the circuit that you assume. Work with a helper so you don't have to run back and forth.

CIRCUITS

A circuit is a closed loop consisting of the circuit breaker (or fuse in older homes), the conductors that carry electricity, and the load, which applies the electricity to produce light, heat, drive motors, or do other work. The breaker protects the circuit by automatically shutting off power to the circuit if it is overloaded. Before you work on a circuit, flip the lever on the circuit breaker to turn off electricity in the circuit.

Electricity travels in a loop from the breaker, through the loads, and back. The outbound conductor is called the hot wire; the return is the neutral. Switches, which open and close the circuit, are wired to the hot conductor. Some dimmers also require a neutral connection.

The size of the wire in a circuit determines its capacity. Capacity is controlled by the circuit breaker, which opens if the capacity is exceeded. A 20-amp circuit is one protected by a 20-amp breaker.

The load on a circuit is the sum of all the devices. A circuit may not be loaded beyond 80 percent of its capacity, according to the National Electric Code. So a 15-amp circuit can have a total load of 12 amps (15 × .8) or less. These limits are more easily expressed in watts for lighting circuits—12 amps = 1,440 watts (12 amps × 120 volts). The limit on a 20-amp circuit is 1,920 watts.

ELECTRICAL WIRING

Conductors are wires—usually copper. The larger its diameter, the more current a wire can carry. Wires carrying too much current for their size overheat and pose a fire hazard.

Wire size is expressed as an American Wire Gauge (AWG, or gauge) number. Lower gauge numbers indicate larger wire diameter. Residential circuits are usually wired with 12- or 14-gauge wire; heavier wire is used for high-capacity dedicated circuits, such as for a range. In a cable, 12-gauge copper wire is rated to carry 25 amps; 14-gauge, 20 amps.

Cable is two or more insulated conductors inside a protective sheathing. Nonmetallic cable (NM) for indoor use—the familiar plastic-covered cable—is often called Romex, a trade name. Some nonmetallic cable is rated for outdoor or underground use. Armored cable (BX or MC) has metal sheathing.

Most homes built now are wired with nonmetallic cable, although some building codes require armored cable. Cable is designated by type and the number and gauge of its conductors: NM 12-2 is nonmetallic cable with two 12-gauge conductors; NM 14-3 contains three 14-gauge conductors. When WG is part of the cable designation, the cable includes a ground wire.

The color of the wire insulation helps you identify conductors. Black or red generally signifies a hot wire; white is neutral, and green (or bare copper) is the ground. In some switch circuits the white wire in a cable serves as a hot lead; in those cases, mark it with black stripes at both ends.

Grounding protects the electrical system by providing an alternate path for the electricity to return to ground. Grounding does not, however, prevent you from being shocked by touching a live wire or socket. Lighting fixtures and controls contain ground wires or contacts that must be connected for safe operation. The bare ground wire in a cable is not considered a conductor.

OUTLET, SWITCH, AND JUNCTION BOXES

Outlet and switch boxes mount in the ceiling or wall and provide a place for the connection and mounting of switches, dimmers, lighting fixtures, and plug receptacles. A junction box encloses wire connections but does not support any device. All electrical connections must be made inside an approved enclosure.

Boxes usually have brackets or ears for attachment to the framing. Several switches or outlets can be installed at one location with multiple-device or gangable boxes.

Wiring connections must be secured by wire nuts, screw terminals, or stab-in (friction) fittings. The cable must also be fastened so that it cannot be pulled out of the box. Many boxes have built-in clamps. Otherwise cable clamps are installed into knock-out holes in boxes. Cable must be stapled or clamped to the framing.

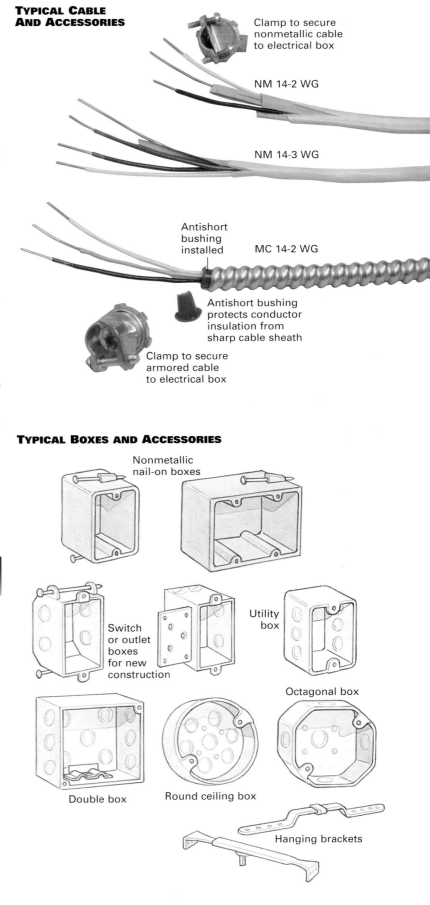

TYPICAL CABLE AND ACCESSORIES

Clamp to secure nonmetallic cable to electrical box

NM 14-2 WG

NM 14-3 WG

Antishort bushing installed

MC 14-2 WG

Antishort bushing protects conductor insulation from sharp cable sheath

Clamp to secure armored cable to electrical box

TYPICAL BOXES AND ACCESSORIES

Nonmetallic nail-on boxes

Switch or outlet boxes for new construction

Utility box

Octagonal box

Double box

Round ceiling box

Hanging brackets

SIMPLE MAINTENANCE

When a light doesn't light up, the most likely problem is a burned-out bulb. Turn off the fixture and tighten the bulb in the socket. Turn the switch back on. If the fixture still does not light, turn the switch back off, and replace the bulb with one of the same type, size, and wattage (or lower wattage).

SWITCH REPLACEMENT

If the fixture does not light with a good bulb in it, the problem is in the fixture, the switch, or the wiring. If only one switch controls the fixture, replacing it will usually fix the problem. Test the switch as shown below. See *Ortho's All About Wiring Basics* for more troubleshooting information, or call an electrician.

You can easily replace the switch in a one-switch circuit. Turn off the power at the circuit breaker, then remove the wall plate from the switch. Take out the two screws that attach the switch to the box. Pull the switch out of the box, and unscrew the terminals to disconnect the wires. (Push a thin screwdriver blade into the slots on the back of the switch to release push-in wire connections.) Attach the wires to the new switch; when there are two wires and two terminals, it doesn't matter which wire goes to which terminal. Reinstall the switch in the box, replace the wall plate, and turn the power back on.

ELECTRICAL PARTS

If the wiring or sockets of a fixture appear burned, have a qualified electrician check the electrical connections and the fixture. If the fixture is a valuable chandelier, an electrician or lighting dealer may be able to properly rewire and repair it. Shut off power at the circuit breaker and cover bare wires for as long as the outlet box is exposed.

A good quality transformer or ballast in a fluorescent fixture should last for at least 10 years when operated properly. Replacing a transformer is a job for an electrician. It may be more practical to replace the entire fixture.

Ballast replacement is easier. Disconnect power to the circuit, and remove the diffuser from the fixture. If you do not see the ballast, remove the metal cover by squeezing the sides of the fixture together.

Write down the model numbers of the ballast and the fluorescent tube to take to your supplier. You may not find the identical model number you are replacing; your supplier can help you select the right one. Replace the ballast using the wiring of the existing one as a guide.

After making firm connections to both terminals, wrap the switch body with electrician's tape. Then, carefully tuck the wires into the box and mount the switch with screws.

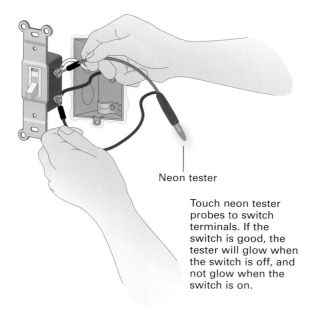

Neon tester

Touch neon tester probes to switch terminals. If the switch is good, the tester will glow when the switch is off, and not glow when the switch is on.

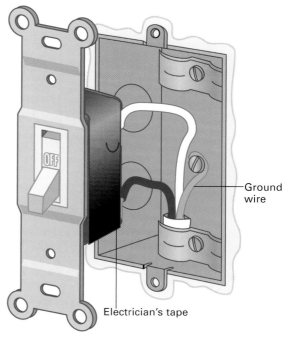

Ground wire

Electrician's tape

OLD OR BROKEN PARTS

Broken diffusers or shades are usually replaceable. However most manufacturers do not retain spare parts after a model is discontinued. A lighting or shade store may have a generic part that will work. Bring the one you want to replace (or a close-up photograph of the fixture) to be sure that the new part will fit. Otherwise replace the entire fixture.

You can usually replace old downlight trim with a new model from the same manufacturer. Note the model of the housing (printed on the label inside the can or near the socket) and bring the old trim to ensure a compatible replacement. Old track lights cannot be repaired easily. Replace them with a new fixture by the same manufacturer. Bring the old fixture to the store to ensure that the new one will fit the track.

TABLE AND FLOOR LAMPS

The power cord of a table lamp or floor lamp may crack over time and should be replaced as soon as you notice the wear. A cracked plug should be replaced immediately; a new one can be wired easily to the end of the cord. To replace the cord entirely, disassemble the lamp to expose the socket and wiring. You may have to remove the harp that holds the shade by squeezing and pulling it out. Slide the shell off the socket and securely connect the replacement cord. The hot lead (the one from the narrow prong on a polarized plug) connects to the switch and the bottom socket contact (the brass screw); the neutral wire connects to the inner shell (the silver screw). Reassemble the lamp.

In a lamp with one socket, the cord goes into the base, runs through the threaded tube, and connects directly to the socket terminals.

Finial

In a lamp with two or more sockets, each socket is wired separately. The wires are connected to the line cord with the wire nuts.

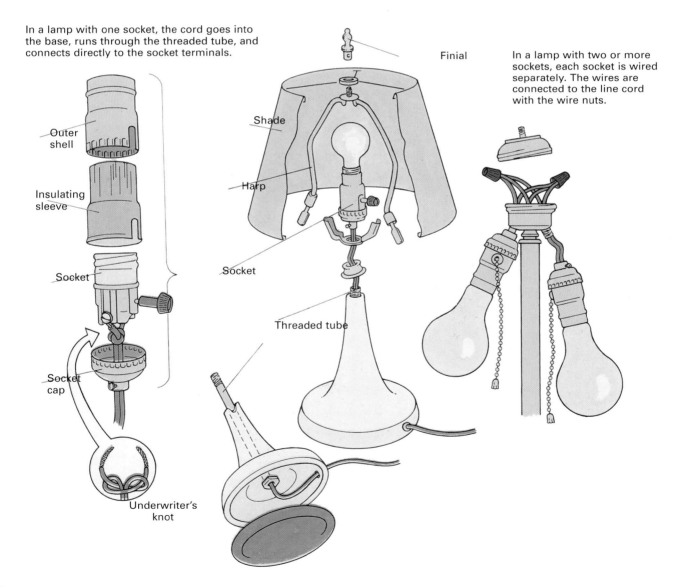

Outer shell

Insulating sleeve

Socket

Socket cap

Underwriter's knot

Shade

Harp

Socket

Threaded tube

INSTALLING CEILING AND WALL FIXTURES

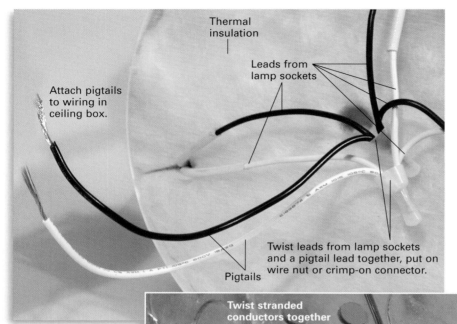

Thermal insulation

Leads from lamp sockets

Attach pigtails to wiring in ceiling box.

Twist leads from lamp sockets and a pigtail lead together, put on wire nut or crimp-on connector.

Pigtails

Splice separate lamp socket leads together with a pigtail to make installation easier (above, right).

To hang the fixture, start the mounting screws into the box ears, then push the round holes in the fixture mounting slots over the screw heads. Turn the fixture to move the screw heads to the ends of the slots, and tighten the screws (below).

Twist stranded conductors together

Pigtails from fixture

Twist pigtail from fixture clockwise around same-color wire in box, put on wire nut.

Installing a new ceiling or wall fixture on an existing junction box is straightforward. A box that was installed during construction will support most fixtures, but a box added later might not support a heavy fixture. A heavy chandelier requires a heavy-duty (50-pound capacity) box that is solidly attached to the framing (see photo, page 94).

Installing a fixture in a new location requires a new outlet box and wiring. See *Ortho's All About Wiring Basics* for information about adding a new box and wiring.

There are different ways to install fixtures, so read the manufacturer's instructions before you start. Some fixtures have to be connected to wiring with insulation rated to withstand a temperature of 90° C. Wiring in older houses is rated for 60° C or 75° C, so you will have to rewire the box or use a different fixture.

■ Shut off the circuit breaker for the fixture before you begin. (See page 86.) Remove the existing fixture, but save the mounting hardware attached to the box in case you need to reuse it. If the house wiring is not color-coded black and white, mark the wire connected to the black lead on the fixture with black electrical tape.

■ Remove the diffuser or other replaceable shades from the new fixture to reduce weight and avoid damage. Connections are usually wired before attaching the fixture to the outlet box. Splice the fixture's black leads to the hot (black) wire in the box and the white leads to the neutral (white) wire, using twist-on wire nuts. If the fixture leads are stranded, wrap them around the solid wire of the supply leads. If both are solid, lay them side by side. Cap with wire nuts by twisting clockwise. Attach the ground (green) lead to the box or the bare ground wire in the box. Tug gently on each connection to make sure they are secure. Carefully fold the wires into the outlet box. Fasten the fixture to the box.

Most fixtures attach to a crossbar or strap fastened to the outlet box. Fixtures usually attach with screws at the corners or to a stud in the middle. Large or long fixtures may have fasteners into wall anchors at the ends or corners. (Holes are generally provided in the housing.) Make sure the fixture is level or correctly aligned before you secure it.

Chandeliers and pendants include a canopy that covers the outlet box. They may use a nipple and hickey, which lets the cord enter the canopy cleanly. When installing the fixture, be sure you slip the canopy over the cord and chain before splicing the wires.

Finally, install the lightbulbs recommended by the manufacturer. Before you attach a diffuser, turn the power on and test the fixture. If the fixture has gaskets to prevent damage from moisture, seat the gasket in the housing before you tighten the diffuser.

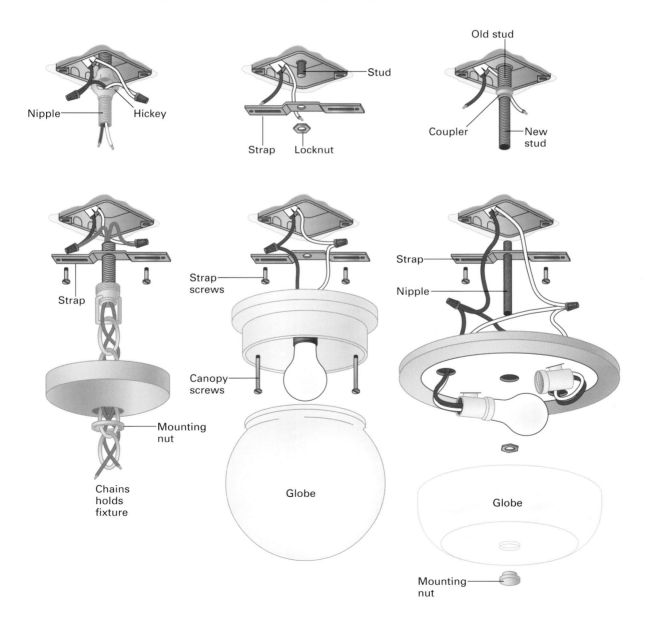

INSTALLING A CEILING FAN

Expanding threaded bracket forces prongs into joist.

Turning threaded sleeve expands bracket

Standard box ear not suitable for mounting fan or heavy ceiling fixture.

Reinforced mounting points

A ceiling fan or chandelier requires a sturdy, solidly mounted box. This kind has reinforced mounting points for the fan or fixture and installs easily through a hole in the finished ceiling.

A fan needs sturdy support—a heavy-duty outlet box firmly secured to the ceiling framing, not to the drywall. If you are not sure how securely mounted an existing box is, give it a strong tug with a pair of pliers. If it moves easily, replace it. Turn off the electricity at the breaker panel before doing any work.

Fan blades that are 8 to 9 feet above the floor cool more effectively. Blades should always be at least 7 feet high. The fan comes with a short down rod for an 8-foot ceiling, but other lengths are available, so you can suspend the fan at any height.

The size of a fan is determined by its blade span, which is the diameter of the sweep, not the actual length of a blade. Place the fan so the tips of the blades are at least 12 inches from any wall. See page 64 for information about selecting a fan.

FAN CONTROLS

Most fans and fan light kits come with pull-cord switches, but control from a wall switch is often more convenient.

■ A dual fan-light control fits into a single switch box and operates the fan and light separately. This requires a three-conductor cable from the switch to the fan outlet box.

■ A more expensive smart control provides separate fan and light control with a two-wire cable outlet by using a communication module that fits in the fan canopy.

■ A wireless remote control device, which is built into some fans, makes it easy to control the fan and light from anywhere in the room, just like your television remote control.

■ A standard wall switch in a two-wire circuit will turn the fan and light on and off together. You can still control fan speed and the light separately with the pull chains.

HANGING THE FAN

Read the manufacturer's directions carefully. Turn off the power at the breaker, and install the bracket on the outlet box. Assemble the fan motor and down rod on the ground. If the fan has an uplight kit, install it, but hang the fan before you install a light kit that goes on the bottom of the fan. Slip the canopy over the down rod, pass the lead wires through the rod, and fasten it to the fan body. If you have installed a longer down rod, put the hanger ball on it. Lift the fan and place the hanger ball into the hanger bracket, inserting the alignment tab in the slot.

Attach the blades to the blade holders. Then fasten the holders to the fan body, working clockwise. Tighten the fasteners finger tight, then secure them all firmly. The blades must be well-balanced or the fan will wobble as it turns. Connect the supply wires to the fan leads. Slide the canopy up to the ceiling.

LIGHT KITS

Bottom-mounted light kits have either a single fitting with a diffuser or a ring of fitters, each with its own glass shade. Connect the wires according to the manufacturer's directions. Carefully tuck them into the splice compartment, and fasten the kit housing to the bottom of the fan. With a single fitting install the lightbulbs and secure the diffuser. With multiple fitters attach the glasses securely by tightening the three thumbscrews, then install the lightbulbs.

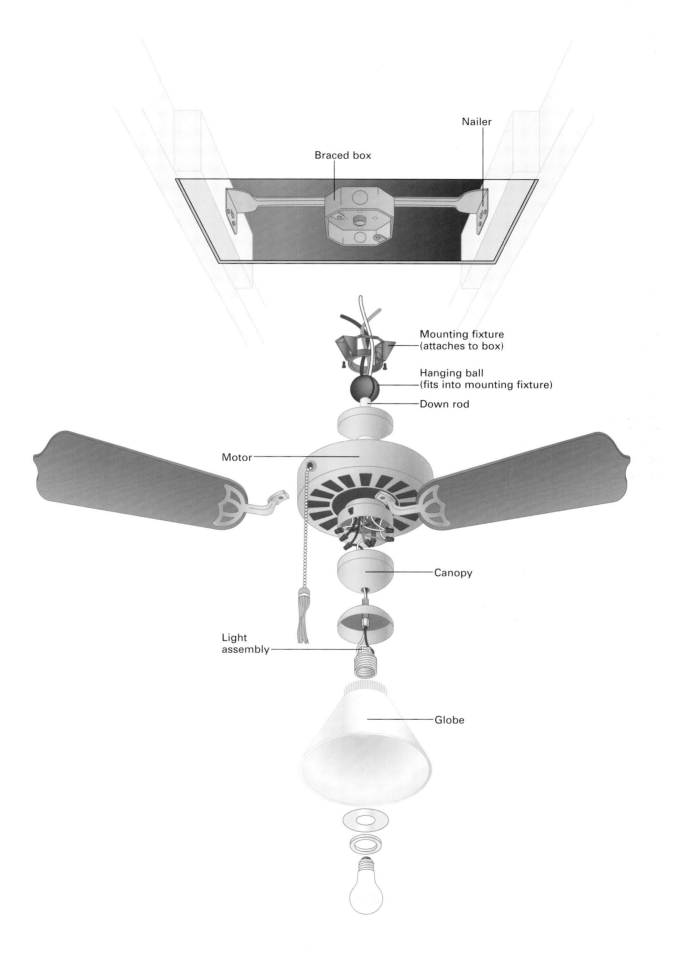

Nailer

Braced box

Mounting fixture
(attaches to box)

Hanging ball
(fits into mounting fixture)

Down rod

Motor

Canopy

Light
assembly

Globe

INSTALLING RECESSED DOWNLIGHTS

Recessed lights with different trims effectively light this room.

Recessed downlights are more complicated to install than a ceiling fixture. But where you have access above the ceiling, the new wiring will not require extensive patching, which will make the job easier. Replacing a ceiling fixture with a recessed downlight may not involve any new wiring at all.

Before starting work turn off power to the circuit at the breaker panel. (See page 86.) Read the manufacturer's instructions carefully because installation varies among fixtures. Only use housings and trims that are UL listed for use together, and observe the lamping directions printed on the fixture label.

CEILING CONDITIONS

The type of fixture housing you need depends on the ceiling. Housings are made for either new construction or remodeling. If the ceiling is unfinished or there is an open attic above it, you can use a new construction housing or frame. If you have to cut a hole in the ceiling and install the fixture from below, you will need a remodel housing.

Most general-purpose downlights need at least 7½ inches above the ceiling, provided by 2×8 joist construction or with smaller joists that have an open attic above. Smaller fixtures are available for depths down to 5 inches. A smaller fixture, such as one with a 3- to 4-inch aperture, will often fit into a tight space, such as a soffit. For still shallower spaces, use special low-voltage downlights or ask your electrical supplier to order conventional ones with ultra-shallow housings. Remodel housings are useful in tight spots, too, because they do not have a large mounting plate.

Downlight housings that are buried in ceiling insulation must be type IC (for insulated ceiling). Type IC housings have an enclosure that is designed to accommodate heat build-up in the fixture caused by the insulation around it. IC housings are identified by prominent markings or labeling.

Housings that are not IC can be used where insulation is at least 3 inches away from the sides of the fixture. Baffles or fences are available to keep insulation clear of the fixture. (Removing insulation is not recommended.) Downlights that are not IC usually take higher-wattage bulbs that are set deeper into the ceiling.

NEW CONSTRUCTION

A new construction housing includes a mounting plate, hanger bars that attach to the ceiling joists, and a junction box (J-box) for splicing the fixture and supply leads. Using your lighting plan, locate all the downlights in the room and mark their positions. This ensures that the completed layout will look well-organized in the ceiling. Also locate the dimmers or switches that will control the downlights. Once you have installed the housing, you will be able to slide it a little from side to side between the joists. Otherwise its position is fixed.

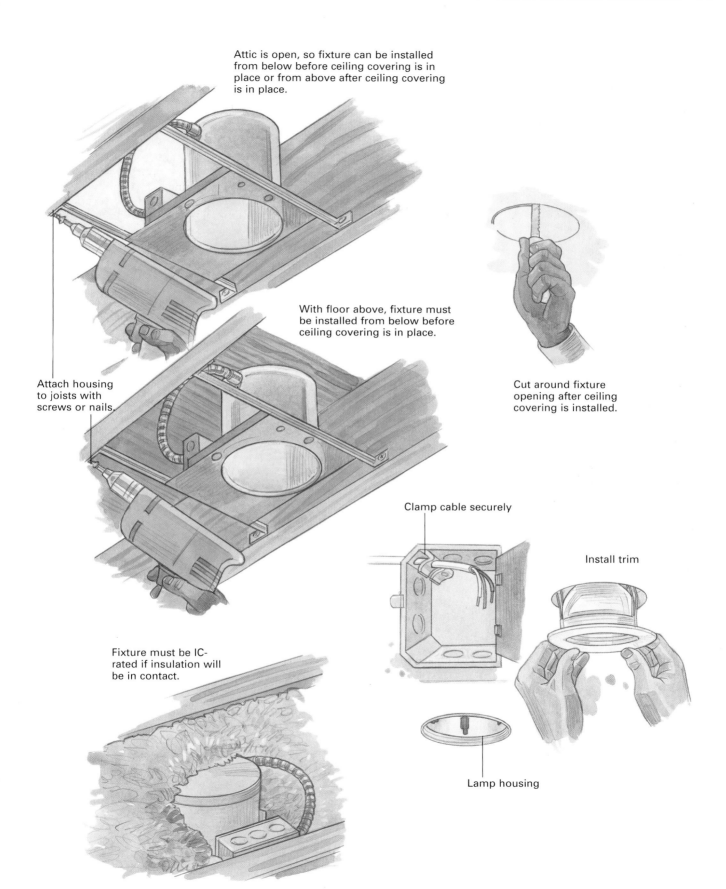

Attic is open, so fixture can be installed from below before ceiling covering is in place or from above after ceiling covering is in place.

With floor above, fixture must be installed from below before ceiling covering is in place.

Attach housing to joists with screws or nails.

Cut around fixture opening after ceiling covering is installed.

Clamp cable securely

Install trim

Fixture must be IC-rated if insulation will be in contact.

Lamp housing

INSTALLING RECESSED DOWNLIGHTS
continued

A remodeler housing makes it easy to install recessed lights in a finished ceiling (see text on opposite page.)

FRAME IN: Prepare the housing for wiring before you mount it in the ceiling. Open the J-box covers, but keep them handy. Many downlight fixtures have an integral cable clamp inside the J-box. Open the knock-out over the cable clamp. If you are running wires through the downlight and on to another one (see the "Wiring" paragraph), open two knock-outs.

Install remodeler (also called old-work) canisters in a finished ceiling. Cut a hole between joists, run new cable, and make new connections in the junction box. The clips hold the fixture in the hole.

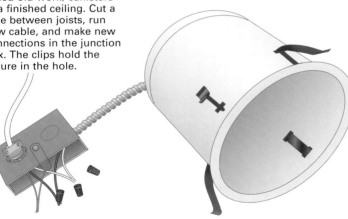

Mount the housing by nailing the ends of the hanger bars to the joists. Position the mounting plate flush with the bottom of the joist. Mount all the housings similarly for uniform appearance in the finished ceiling. Slide the housings until they are correctly aligned with each other and lock the bars to the frame with the hardware provided or with a sheet metal screw.

WIRING: It is easiest to bring power first to the switch box, then to the first downlight. (See the topmost illustration on page 104.) Run wires from the first downlight to the next one, and so forth. With three-way controls it is usually simpler to wire the circuit as shown at the top right on page 105. When running cable, drill holes at least 1½ inches from the edge of the joist. Secure the cable loosely until you have finished making all the connections. Staple the cable within 12 inches of the J-box and every 3 feet along its run.

Insert the cable through the knock-out and cable clamp. Remove several inches of sheathing and about ½ inch of insulation from the conductors. Connect the black fixture wire to the hot conductor and the white wire to the neutral. Connect the ground wires. Pull all but 1 inch of the sheathed cable out of the J-box, and tighten the cable clamp. Install a lightbulb and check the installation.

FINISH THE CEILING: Finishing the ceiling with drywall is a two-person job that will take longer than installing the downlights. The key to a professional-looking job is to cut a neat hole in the right place. You can either cut the drywall on the floor or after you have fastened it to the ceiling; cutting before hanging the ceiling is easier, but calls for careful measurements. Measure the position of the hole from the edge of the installed sheet. Draw an accurate circle ¼ inch larger than the opening of the downlight. Cut it cleanly; a rotary hole saw does a better job than a drywall handsaw.

To cut the hole after the ceiling is in place, mark the center of the downlight location on

Customize the appearance of your lights as well as the way the cast light by choosing from a variety of trim options.

Trim with lens to cover a standard light bulb

Adjustable eyeball trim

Reflector cone to intensify light

the floor, using a plumb bob. When the ceiling is installed, use the plumb bob to transfer the mark to the ceiling. Cut from the center to the edge of the opening in the downlight, then draw the circular cutting line. Cut neatly around the outside of the downlight flange. A rotary saw works best because the mounting frame limits the stroke of a straight saw blade.

ADD THE TRIM: Install downlight trim after painting the ceiling. The socket mounts to a plate at the top of the housing or can in some downlights. The setting guide in the fixture shows the correct position for the trim you will install.

Springs usually hook into slots in the housing to hold the trim. Baffle and reflector trims typically include a separate plastic ring to cover the gap between the edge of the hole and the fixture. Slip the ring into place before attaching the springs.

In some downlights the socket attaches directly to the trim, which is then held by friction clips. In this case snap the socket onto the trim and push up the assembly until the friction clips grip it tightly. Rotate the installed trim clockwise slightly to tighten it against the ceiling.

REMODELING

Remodeling means installing a downlight in a completed ceiling. Replacing a surface-mounted fixture with a recessed one is relatively easy. The basic steps are the same as for new construction, shown on the previous pages. Instead of a new-construction housing, use a remodeler housing. A few installation details are different.

Turn off the power and remove the existing fixture. Disconnect the supply leads from the existing outlet box and remove it. Carefully cut an opening for the new fixture, using the template provided with it (or trace the circle using the bottom edge of the housing). Make the hole fit the fixture as tightly as possible.

Pull the supply cable through the hole in the ceiling and wire it into the J-box on the downlight. Push the housing back up into the ceiling and clamp it in place. Spring clips that are pressed down with the tip of a screwdriver hold most remodel housings in place by sandwiching the ceiling between the clips and the flange on the fixture. Screw in the lightbulb, test the fixture, and install the finishing trim. You can install a series of downlights in the same way, wiring them together.

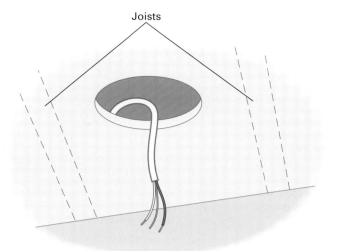

Joists

Cut the hole carefully so the canister will fit tightly. Run cable, and connect it to the canister's electrical box.

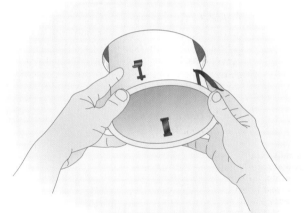

Push the canister up tight against the ceiling, and push on each of the four clips until they clamp down tight. Install the trim and light bulb.

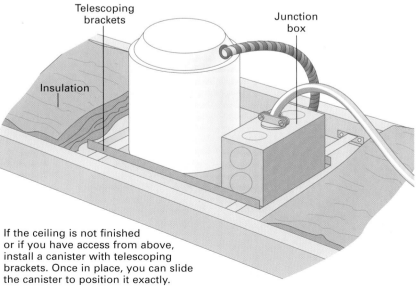

Telescoping brackets

Junction box

Insulation

If the ceiling is not finished or if you have access from above, install a canister with telescoping brackets. Once in place, you can slide the canister to position it exactly.

INSTALLING TRACK LIGHTING

Track lighting simplifies many room lighting projects because you can install several fixtures without running a lot of new wiring. You can connect the track to an existing outlet box, run additional track sections where you want them, then clip on the fixtures.

A complete installation requires the appropriate track sections, couplers to join the sections, pattern connectors for corner or junctions, a feed connection, and the lighting fixtures. Components are available separately or in starter kits from lighting dealers or home centers. The dealer can help you select compatible parts.

Before installation open all packaging and read the manufacturer's instructions. Install track lighting only in dry locations, at least 5 feet above the floor. Keep fixtures at least 6 inches away from curtains or other combustible materials. The only devices you should connect to the track are those provided by the track manufacturer for the specific track that you have.

EXISTING CEILING AND OUTLET BOX

First plan the track layout. To light walls or art hanging on them, locate the track 24 to 30 inches from the wall. If the track is farther away, the spotlights may shine into the eyes of people close to the wall. To hang pendants over a table or counter, center the track over the surface.

The outlet box usually is not aligned with the track, so create a T or L pattern to run a section of the track to the box. Make a diagram of the layout.

Measure each leg of the pattern on the ceiling. Divide each leg into the appropriate lengths of track. (Track sections are usually furnished in nominal 2-, 4-, and 8-foot lengths.) Note the lengths on your material list and your layout diagram. You can cut the track sections to length, but you cannot reuse short cutoff ends.

Determine how many couplers you will need to join the sections of track. Use a mini-coupler for a straight joint between two sections of track and the appropriate pattern connector for an L or T.

Track that ends at the outlet box connects to the wiring with a live-end feed, which plugs into the end of the track. If the track passes over the outlet box, it connects with a floating or saddle feed, which fits over the track. Power connectors usually come with a canopy cover for the box. Covers for the dead ends of the track are furnished with each section.

Unlimited possibilities for track layout and a wide range of available fixtures make track lighting a versatile tool for room lighting.

FLOATING FEED

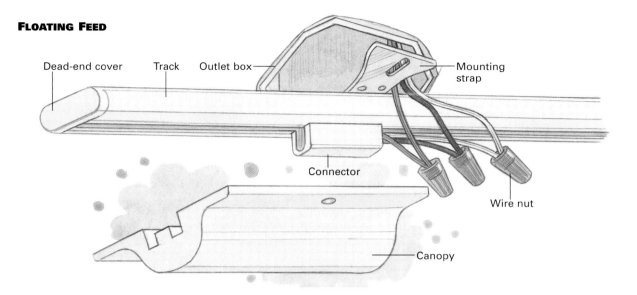

Dead-end cover   Track   Outlet box   Mounting strap

Connector

Wire nut

Canopy

Snap a chalk line on the ceiling to mark the track path. Make sure it is parallel to the wall and squarely aligned in the room.

Turn off power to the outlet box at the breaker panel. Open the track packaging and set aside the mounting hardware. Begin installing track at the outlet box. Attach the mounting hardware for the power feed to the outlet box. Remove the cover of the live-end feed and attach the lead wires to the screw terminals. (Installation of a floating feed is described on page 102.) Tuck the lead wires back into the outlet box. Be sure the live end is pointing the right way, then fasten it to the mounting strap, inserting the canopy cover, if it is separate.

Place the first section of track against the ceiling and push one end over the live-end feed until it connects securely. Fasten the track to the ceiling, using the hardware furnished with the track. To extend the track run, insert a mini-coupler, then attach the next section. A bead or groove on the face indicates the track's hot/neutral polarity—maintain polarity as you install each new section of track. Continue for all lengths of track and pattern connectors. Attach a dead-end cover at any exposed track end.

If you have to cut a section of track to length, measure and cut it just before you install it so you'll be sure that the dimensions are exact. Cut the track with a hacksaw, and remove any burrs. Make cuts in track sections that fall at the end of the run, away from the live end. If you must insert a mini-coupler, live-end, or pattern connector into a cut track end, be sure that the track conductors make clean contact.

LIVE-END FEED

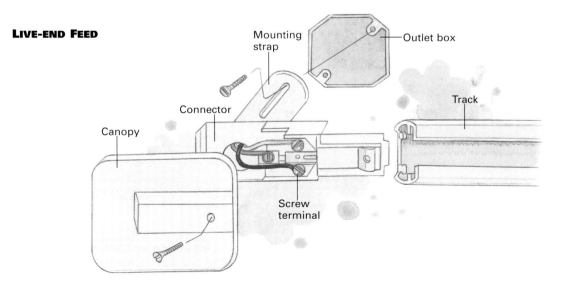

Mounting strap   Outlet box

Connector   Track

Canopy

Screw terminal

INSTALLING TRACK LIGHTING
continued

DIRECT FEED FROM TOP

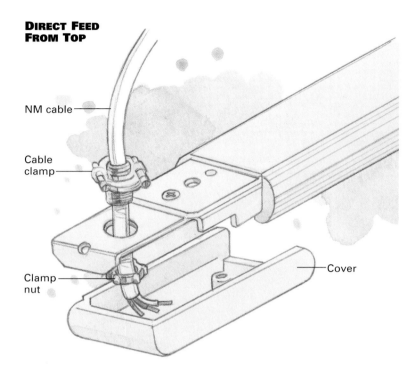

NM cable

Cable clamp

Clamp nut

Cover

FLOATING OR SADDLE FEED

The basic technique is the same as a live-end feed. At the outlet box install the mounting hardware and splice the supply leads to the wires from the power adapter. Then install the first section of track over the outlet box. When the track is in place, twist the power adapter into the track and cover the outlet box with the canopy.

Most pattern connectors also provide for an electrical feed. This lets you feed to the corner of an L or T pattern either through an outlet box or directly, without using an additional live end at that point.

DIRECT FEED

Where there is no convenient outlet box, you can wire track directly to a cable from a switch, as shown *above* and *below*. A direct feed from the top makes a cleaner looking installation, but you'll need to run cable from the switch to the top of the live-end connector. No canopy cover is required. You'll have to hide the cable for a feed from the end.

For the top-cable feed, position the track on the ceiling and mark the location of the cable hole in the live-end connector. Drill a

DIRECT FEED FROM END

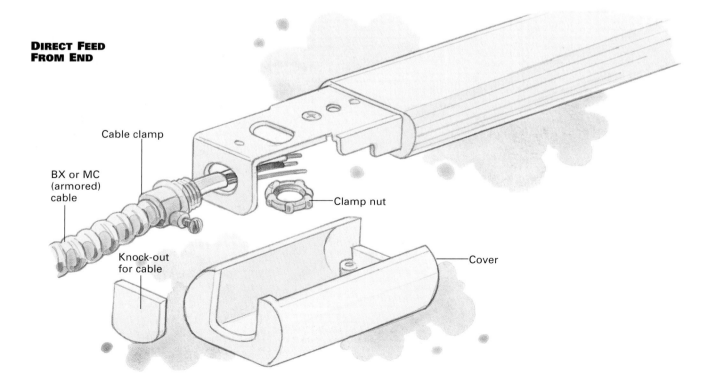

Cable clamp

BX or MC (armored) cable

Clamp nut

Knock-out for cable

Cover

¾- or 1-inch hole in the ceiling, then fish the cable to the switch box. (See Ortho's *All About Wiring Basics* for more information.) For either type of feed, remove 2 inches of the cable sheathing and strip ¾ inch of the conductors. Form the conductors into a loop and attach them to the screw terminals. Attach a ⅜-inch BX or Romex clamp to the end of the cable. Attach the cable clamp and secure the wires.

Measure from the wall, and mark a light pencil line parallel to it.

NEW CONSTRUCTION

Install track on a new ceiling with either an outlet box or using the direct-feed method. Install the track after the ceiling is enclosed.

ATTACHING TRACK FIXTURES

Install bulbs in the fixtures before installation. Attach the fixtures to the track—they usually twist in, making both the electrical and mechanical connections. (Some models include a switch on the attachment fitting.) Follow the manufacturer's directions to ensure that the fixture maintains the correct polarity.

Attach the track to the connector unit, and secure it to the ceiling with screws and anchors. Press the end plug in place. Twist individual lights into track.

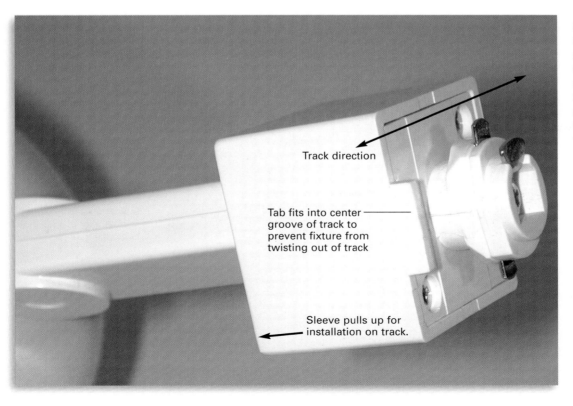

Metal lugs on this fixture base make electrical contact with conductors in the track. The base fits into the track only one way.

Track direction

Tab fits into center groove of track to prevent fixture from twisting out of track

Sleeve pulls up for installation on track.

INSTALLING SWITCHES AND DIMMERS

Each layer of lighting in a room should have a separate dimmer or switch. This lets you select which lights are on and allows you to adjust their intensity to set a scene. When you add new lighting fixtures to a room, add the appropriate control at the same time. Use three-way devices in a large room or a space with multiple entries. Mount the new switch boxes at the same height as the old ones (48 inches is typical). Before opening any existing switch box or installing any cable, shut off power at the breaker panel.

If you are not experienced in electrical repairs, hire a licensed electrician. It's often better to have an electrician install central control and dimming systems, fluorescent dimmers, or other complex arrangements.

NEW SINGLE-POLE SWITCH

Single-pole switches have two terminals. Most use screw terminals; a few have push-in connections. The switch connects to the hot conductor. When the switch is open, the circuit is interrupted and the lights are off. When the switch is closed, the circuit is completed and the lights are on.

Run the cable into the box and clamp it, leaving several inches of the leads exposed. Strip insulation from the leads, measuring against the guide on the back of the switch or following the instructions that come with the dimmer. Connect the hot (black) wires to the terminals of the switch. Splice the neutral (white) conductors together. Connect the ground wires to the box or the switch. (The switch may not be grounded.) Wrap the switch with electrical tape to cover the screw terminals. Dimmers have wire leads for connections, rather than terminals. Follow the manufacturer's directions for making the connection. Fasten the control to the box with screws, taking care to keep it plumb.

NEW THREE-WAY CONTROL

Three-way switches have three terminals; two are brass, one is silver or another color. (Green is for the ground.) The silver (or nonbrass) terminal is called the *common* terminal and is usually marked.

All three-way switches are wired in the same way. The hot lead from the breaker panel connects to the common terminal on one switch. The hot lead to the fixture connects to the common terminal of the other switch. The two other terminals on both of the other switches are connected together by wires, called *travelers*.

The diagrams on the opposite page show wiring for different locations of the power supply, switches, and fixture. In some circuits the white wire becomes a hot lead; mark the ends black to identify it. If you use three-conductor cable throughout cap the unused lead with a wire nut.

SINGLE-POLE SWITCH, POWER TO SWITCH

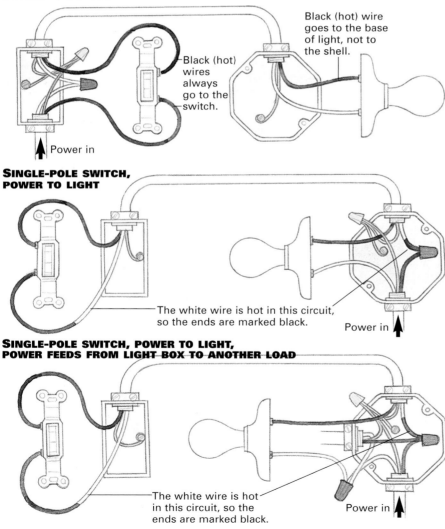

Black (hot) wires always go to the switch.

Black (hot) wire goes to the base of light, not to the shell.

Power in

SINGLE-POLE SWITCH, POWER TO LIGHT

The white wire is hot in this circuit, so the ends are marked black.

Power in

SINGLE-POLE SWITCH, POWER TO LIGHT, POWER FEEDS FROM LIGHT BOX TO ANOTHER LOAD

The white wire is hot in this circuit, so the ends are marked black.

Power in

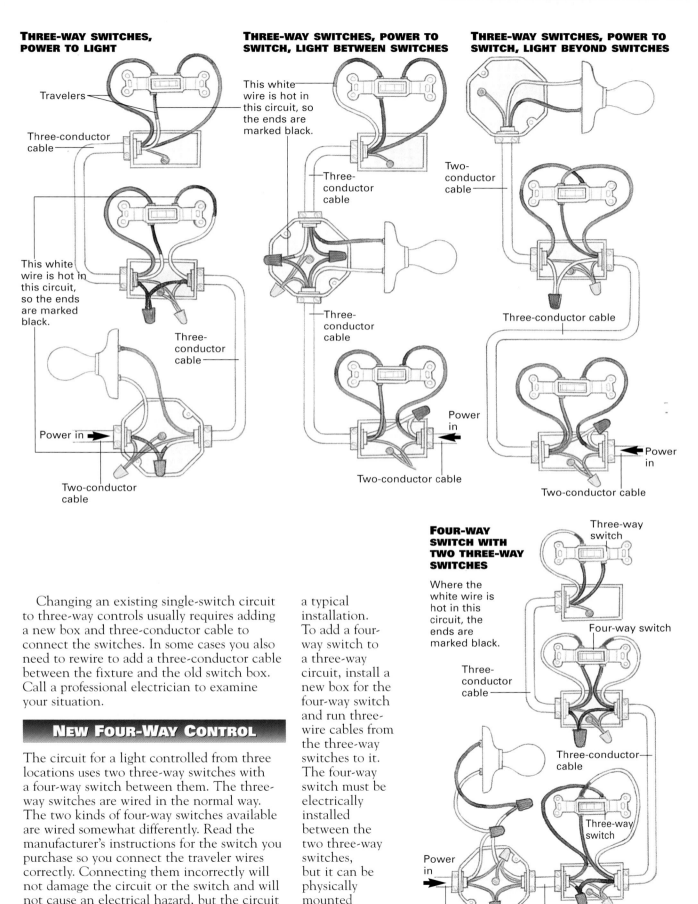

THREE-WAY SWITCHES, POWER TO LIGHT

Travelers

Three-conductor cable

This white wire is hot in this circuit, so the ends are marked black.

Power in ►

Two-conductor cable

Three-conductor cable

THREE-WAY SWITCHES, POWER TO SWITCH, LIGHT BETWEEN SWITCHES

This white wire is hot in this circuit, so the ends are marked black.

Three-conductor cable

Three-conductor cable

Power in ◄

Two-conductor cable

THREE-WAY SWITCHES, POWER TO SWITCH, LIGHT BEYOND SWITCHES

Two-conductor cable

Three-conductor cable

Three-conductor cable

◄ Power in

Two-conductor cable

Changing an existing single-switch circuit to three-way controls usually requires adding a new box and three-conductor cable to connect the switches. In some cases you also need to rewire to add a three-conductor cable between the fixture and the old switch box. Call a professional electrician to examine your situation.

NEW FOUR-WAY CONTROL

The circuit for a light controlled from three locations uses two three-way switches with a four-way switch between them. The three-way switches are wired in the normal way. The two kinds of four-way switches available are wired somewhat differently. Read the manufacturer's instructions for the switch you purchase so you connect the traveler wires correctly. Connecting them incorrectly will not damage the circuit or the switch and will not cause an electrical hazard, but the circuit will not work. The illustration *at right* shows

a typical installation. To add a four-way switch to a three-way circuit, install a new box for the four-way switch and run three-wire cables from the three-way switches to it. The four-way switch must be electrically installed between the two three-way switches, but it can be physically mounted anywhere.

FOUR-WAY SWITCH WITH TWO THREE-WAY SWITCHES

Where the white wire is hot in this circuit, the ends are marked black.

Three-way switch

Four-way switch

Three-conductor cable

Three-conductor cable

Three-way switch

Power in ►

Two-conductor cable

Two-conductor cable

INSTALLING SWITCHES AND DIMMERS
continued

SELECTING A DIMMER

Preset dimmers work well for the majority of applications, but ones that aren't preset and digital models are also available. (See page 31.) The first step in selection is to identify the type of light you want to dim—incandescent, low-voltage incandescent with magnetic transformer, or low-voltage with electronic transformer. If you do not know the kind of transformer, look at the fixture. Small and lightweight, electronic transformers are used in most low-voltage track fixtures and undercabinet task lights. Magnetic transformers are large and heavy. They are used in most low-voltage downlights and systems of 150 watts or more.

Add up the wattage of the bulbs the dimmer will control. Use a dimmer that is rated for the type and wattage of the load you plan to control. (Add 20 percent to the wattage of bulbs driven by magnetic transformers to account for power consumed by the transformer.) Do not exceed the dimmer's wattage capacity.

REPLACING A SWITCH WITH A DIMMER

To replace a switch with a dimmer, determine whether the existing switch is a single-pole or three-way device. To do that, turn off the power at the breaker panel. Remove the switch faceplate, remove the switch mounting screws, and pull the switch out of the box to examine the wires. If the switch has two terminals with insulated wires connected to them, it is a single-pole switch. A three-way switch has three insulated wires connected to three terminals and is always in a circuit with another three-way switch.

Replace a single-pole switch with a single-pole dimmer and a three-way (three-pole) switch with a three-way dimmer. Wiring connections vary among dimmer types; read the manufacturer's directions. Before starting any switch replacement, make sure the power is turned off at the circuit breaker.

SINGLE-POLE DIMMER: Remove the existing switch. Cut off the looped ends on the wires and strip off insulation to expose the conductor to the length specified. If the dimmer has two black leads, splice them to the two black wires. If the dimmer has leads of different colors, splice the black lead to the wire from the breaker. Splice the colored one to the fixture wire. Connect the ground wire. Fold and tuck the wires into the box and fasten the dimmer in place.

THREE-WAY DIMMER: For three-way operation replace one of the three-way switches with a three-way dimmer. Before removing the switch, tag the wire connected to the common terminal (marked on the switch) with a piece of tape. Strip the wires, as above. Splice the

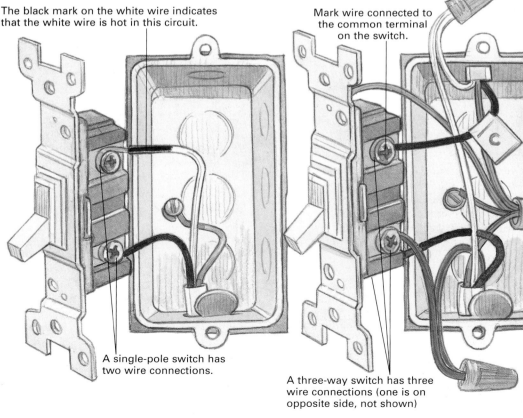

SINGLE-POLE SWITCH

The black mark on the white wire indicates that the white wire is hot in this circuit.

A single-pole switch has two wire connections.

THREE-WAY SWITCH

Mark wire connected to the common terminal on the switch.

A three-way switch has three wire connections (one is on opposite side, not shown)

black lead from the dimmer to the tagged wire, then remove the tag. Splice the remaining leads to the wires, following the manufacturer's instructions. Complete the installation as discussed above.

NEUTRAL CONNECTION: Some dimmers must be connected to the circuit's neutral lead for proper operation. (The manufacturer's instructions will specify this.) If there is no neutral lead in the switch box (check both boxes in a three-way circuit), ask your dealer if another type of dimmer will work. Otherwise rewire the circuit to provide a neutral lead. You may be making four or five connections (supply, load, neutral, ground, and three-way), so install a deep switch box, which provides more room.

DIMMER WITH REMOTE CONTROL: Some dimmers have electronic remote controls that allow operation from the other location in a three-way circuit. The remote usually looks like a rocker switch or an electronic switch, but it is a special-purpose device. Read the manufacturer's instructions to determine when a special remote is required. Purchase a remote that is compatible with your dimmer, and install it in place of the second three-way switch. Wiring is similar to dimmer wiring; follow the manufacturer's instructions. Leave both the dimmer and the remote exposed while you work so you can easily identify the wiring.

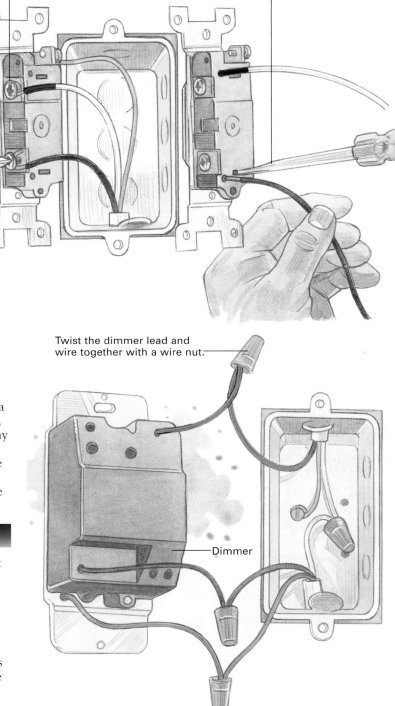

Loosen screws to remove wires from terminals.

Push screwdriver tip into release slot to remove wires from backwired devices.

Twist the dimmer lead and wire together with a wire nut.

Dimmer

FACEPLATES

Switches and most dimmers are sold without the faceplate that covers the switch box. Toggle-style devices use a standard toggle-switch plate. Rocker and touch-pad devices use the designer-style plate that has a large rectangular opening. Both types screw into the mounting bracket of the control device. A screwless designer-style faceplate improves the appearance of the control. To install one attach the concealed support bracket to the dimmer, then snap on the faceplate.

MULTI-GANG INSTALLATION

You can install multiple switches in one location with a wall box made for the purpose. Some single boxes can be ganged (joined to make a box for multiple devices). You can also install several dimmers in longer wall boxes, but check the spacing requirements in the manufacturer's instructions. Putting the dimmers closer together means you must remove part of the heat sink built into the support strap of the dimmer. That reduces the wattage capacity of the dimmer, as indicated in the instructions. Faceplates are available for a number of combinations. You can assemble custom configurations with modular faceplates.

GLOSSARY

COLOR-RENDERING INDEX: The CRI indicates how a light source affects the appearance of colors. On the 1-to-100 scale, 100 indicates no color shift. Objects may look unnatural under lights with a low CRI.

COLOR TEMPERATURE: Measurement of the color warmth of a light source, measured on the Kelvin scale. Sources below 3200° K are usually considered warm; those above 4000° K are considered cool.

CONDUCTOR: The part of a circuit that carries electricity; an electrical wire.

CONTRAST: The variance between light and dark elements.

CURRENT: The flow of electricity, measured in amps.

DECORATIVE LIGHTING: Exposed fixtures that mount on junction box in a wall or ceiling.

DIFFUSER: A translucent shade that spreads or softens light.

DIMMER: A device to control the intensity of a light source.

DIRECT LIGHT: Light that reaches a surface without reflecting off another surface.

DOWNLIGHTING: Light directed down onto an object or surface.

FLOODLIGHT: A lighting fixture that projects a broad beam of light.

FLUORESCENT LAMP: A bulb that produces light by causing an internal phosphor coating to glow.

FOOT-CANDLE: A unit for measuring light falling on a surface; equal to 1 lumen per square foot.

FOUR-WAY SWITCH: Used in conjunction with two three-way switches to control a single light from three points.

GLARE: Excessively harsh or bright light.

GLOW: Soft spread of light from a luminous object, such as a fixture with a diffused globe.

GLOBE: A spherical lamp or diffuser.

ACCENT LIGHTING: Light that focuses attention on an object or surface.

AMBIENT LIGHTING: Light that provides general illumination in a room.

AMP: Shortened form of *ampere*, the unit for measuring the flow of electrical current.

ARCHITECTURAL LIGHTING: Lighting fixtures that are built into a structure.

BEAM: Concentrated light that shines directly onto an object or surface.

CABLE: Several insulated conductors contained in a metallic (BX, MC) or plastic (NM) sheathing.

CIRCUIT: A path for electrical current.

CIRCUIT BREAKER: A device that shuts off power in a circuit when the maximum load is exceeded. It may also be shut off manually so you can safely work on the wiring.

GRAZING LIGHT: Light that strikes a surface at an acute angle; often used to highlight the texture of a surface.

HALOGEN LAMP: An incandescent lightbulb that contains halogen vapor and operates at a high temperature.

HID LAMP: A high-intensity discharge light source, such as mercury or sodium lamps.

ILLUMINATOR: The light source for a fiber-optic system; may contain filters or a rotating color wheel to introduce color into the light.

INCANDESCENT LAMP: A bulb that produces light when the flow of electricity heats a thin filament wire until it glows or incandesces.

INDIRECT LIGHT: Light that reflects off another surface before reaching an object or a surface.

INTENSITY: The amount of light emitted by a source and the amount that ultimately reaches an object or surface.

LAMP: An electric light source; also the popular name for a portable fixture.

LED: Light-emitting diode; a small low-power light source.

LOAD: The part of a circuit that produces light, heat, or motion; the lamp in a lighting circuit.

LOAD CENTER: A panel that distributes electricity through circuit breakers to various circuits in a house.

LOW-VOLTAGE LIGHTING: Lighting that operates at less than line voltage (110–120 volts), often 12 volts.

LUMEN: A measure of light output. One lumen of light uniformly distributed over 1 square foot of surface provides 1 foot-candle of illuminance.

NEC: National Electrical Code. A set of rules for installing wiring and devices.

OUTDOOR LIGHTING: Lighting for safety, security, or aesthetics outside the house.

OUTLET BOX: A steel or plastic housing that holds an electrical device and encloses the electrical connections to the device, usually mounted to the structure of a building. Also known as a *junction box*.

PORTABLE: A lighting fixture not attached to a structure, often called a table lamp or floor lamp.

POWER: Work performed by electricity, measured in watts.

PRIMARY: The input side of a transformer.

REFLECTIVITY: The amount of light that an object reflects is determined by its reflectivity, a technical term for its lightness.

SECONDARY: The output side of a transformer.

SINGLE-POLE SWITCH: A switch used to control a light from a single point.

SPARKLE: Reflections of light from objects such as crystal or tableware.

SPOTLIGHT: A lighting fixture that projects a narrow beam of light.

TASK LIGHTING: Illumination on a work area.

THREE-WAY SWITCH: Used in pairs to control a light from two points.

TORCHÉRE: A floor lamp that shines up.

TRANSFORMER: A device that changes the voltage in an AC circuit.

UL: Underwriters Laboratories. A testing and certification organization.

UPLIGHTING: Light directed up onto an object or surface, such as a ceiling.

VOLT: The unit for measuring electrical force.

VOLTAGE DROP: The reduction in voltage because of resistance in the conductor. Voltage drop can reduce light output.

WASH OF LIGHT: Light that strikes a surface obliquely, lighting it evenly.

WATT: A measure of electrical power; voltage multiplied by amperage. A common way to indicate relative brightness of light sources.

XENON LAMP: An incandescent bulb contains xenon gas; often used in low-voltage lights.

INDEX

METRIC CONVERSIONS

U.S. Units to Metric Equivalents			Metric Units to U.S. Equivalents		
To Convert From	Multiply By	To Get	To Convert From	Multiply By	To Get
Inches	25.4	Millimeters	Millimeters	0.0394	Inches
Inches	2.54	Centimeters	Centimeters	0.3937	Inches
Feet	30.48	Centimeters	Centimeters	0.0328	Feet
Feet	0.3048	Meters	Meters	3.2808	Feet
Yards	0.9144	Meters	Meters	1.0936	Yards
Square inches	6.4516	Square centimeters	Square centimeters	0.1550	Square inches
Square feet	0.0929	Square meters	Square meters	10.764	Square feet
Square yards	0.8361	Square meters	Square meters	1.1960	Square yards
Acres	0.4047	Hectares	Hectares	2.4711	Acres
Cubic inches	16.387	Cubic centimeters	Cubic centimeters	0.0610	Cubic inches
Cubic feet	0.0283	Cubic meters	Cubic meters	35.315	Cubic feet
Cubic feet	28.316	Liters	Liters	0.0353	Cubic feet
Cubic yards	0.7646	Cubic meters	Cubic meters	1.308	Cubic yards
Cubic yards	764.55	Liters	Liters	0.0013	Cubic yards

To convert from degrees Fahrenheit (F) to degrees Celsius (C), first subtract 32, then multiply by ⅝.

To convert from degrees Celsius to degrees Fahrenheit, multiply by ⅘, then add 32.